INDIANA SESQUICENTENNIAL POETS

INDIANA SESQUICENTENNIAL POETS

Thomas H. Wetmore
Editor

BALL STATE UNIVERSITY
Muncie, Indiana
1967

Library of Congress Catalog Card Number: 67-64642

CONTENTS

Sesquicentennial Poets

Honorable Mention

136	Terry Cauley	Bloomington
139	Louis J. Foerderer	Indianapolis
143	Alice Elizabeth Frain	Indianapolis
146	Joyce Gulleson	Indianapolis
147	Emma Blosser Hartzler	Goshen
150	Earl Hughes	Mitchell
155	John Pratt	Muncie
158	Mary Roe	Winchester
162	Mary D. Sare	Indianapolis
164	Cordelia Spitzer	Kokomo
165	Ruth Torbert	Indianapolis
171	Margaret Trusler	Indianapolis

Selected Poems by Other Entrants

174	George W. Allison	Hanover
175	Warren Andrew	Indianapolis
176	Rowena Applegate	Indianapolis
177	Edward Lee Barker	Peru
178	Bob Basler, Jr.	Indianapolis
178	Riley Bertram	Franklin
180	Cliff Byers, Jr.	Fort Wayne
182	Timotheus H. Carson	Indianapolis
184	Patricia Anna Constable	Columbus
185	Lois Anne Cowles	Indianapolis
187	Winifred E. Eads	Indianapolis
189	Mary E. Gibson	Indianapolis
191	Jay Gould	Fort Wayne
192	Constance Grogan	New Whiteland
193	Meredith R. Haskett	Mooresville
193	Grant Henderson	Greensburg
194	James C. Jewell	Terre Haute
195	Steven Kern	Indianapolis

Selected Humorous Entries

FOREWORD

The Indiana College English Association is pleased to present poems by the winners in the competition to select outstanding Indiana Sesquicentennial poets: first place, Constance Hunting; second place, Jared Carter and David F. Gladish; third place, Ray Mizer; fourth place, Arnold Lazarus, Joseph Colin Murphey, Michael J. Phillips, Malcolm M. Sedam, and Daisy Stieber Squadra; fifth place, Willis Barnstone and Thomas N. Meek; and sixth place, Elizabeth Behnke, Mildred Leisure Irvin, Jeanne Eagles McCormack, and Frances Brown Price. Also included are selections from those who received honorable mention and individual poems from a number of other entrants.

This volume is the product of much institutional and individual cooperation. In the summer of 1966, Professor Walter L. Fertig, president of the Indiana College English Association, petitioned the Indiana Sesquicentennial Commission to sanction competition to discover outstanding Indiana poets. The Commission, under the chairmanship of Professor Donald F. Carmony, sanctioned the competition and named the Indiana College English Association as sponsor.

Professor Fertig designated the editor of this volume as chairman to serve with a panel of judges consisting of the following seven professors of English: Walter Fertig, Wabash College; Melvin Plotinski, Indiana University; Lewis Rosenthal, Butler University; Walter Sanders, Valparaiso University; Joseph Satterwhite, Ball State University; George Smock, Indiana State University; and Felix Stefanile, Purdue University.

The chairman received twelve poems each from 177 poets. He assigned each entrant a number and submitted the poems to the judges with only the number identification. All seven judges selected the top ten poets and ranked them. Besides ranking the poets, they indicated poems which they thought might be considered for publication.

The editor gratefully acknowledges indebtedness to Mrs. Rowena Applegate of Indianapolis, who suggested the competition; to the seven judges, who carefully read the 2124 entries; and to Vice-President Richard W. Burkhardt of Ball State University, who encouraged the publication of the poems and secured the necessary financial support. He is also grateful to Bayne Wetmore, who suggested the theme and general design for the art work, and to Ronald McVey, the artist who so successfully captured this Indiana Sesquicentennial theme in his illustrations.

Thomas H. Wetmore

CONSTANCE HUNTING

Miss Dickinson

She cut the wrapping paper neatly
into rectangles—no one would ask why,
it was New England's way—you saved
against the day. No matter what

the parcel had contained,
butcher's delivery, book
by some downstate sage, immediate
scissors flamed in her pocket.

New England makes its women
strange now and then—they take
to cats, or murder, often
in multiples; but she,

compound of thrift and greed
in primstitched white, preferred
to catechize mortality
in the side yard, and afterward

scratched on what leaves
(maple, perhaps, or elm)
only an oracle of Amherst,
Massachusetts, could command

the gist of the matter. Thrift
may have special uses—
likely the household's
other women saved the string.

Constance Hunting

Afternoon of a Contemporary Poet

The friend who has a gall bladder
phones: the operation to be done
on Saturday. But only look—
the grand piano, suffering what indignities,
is rolling up the walk,
supported by three men. Crack crack
and crack the floors says, terrified.
"Do all floors do this in all houses
where you deliver pianos?"
"No, lady."
My son arrives from school, bearing a few
sad fallen leaves (it has rained since)
which we must enter immediately in
the dictionary. It is quite full already,
but he does not mind that. And out of these
will spin the tenuous free-wheeling web
of image, while from the top
of the refrigerator the Siamese,
vulture-like, brooding on fancied wrongs,
stares like the ultimate metaphor at five o'clock.

Constance Hunting

City Park: Spring

On Sunday afternoon the girls
in their thin silk dresses walk out lithe
bellies swaying bottoms swinging
and path-proud pigeons creak aside
pretending with a superb
unnoticed condescension not to take
cognizance
but the old benched men
sifting the ashes of yesterday's
newspapers sense behind their eyeballs
distant burning signals of countries long
unvisited while sailors stealthily
detach themselves from chewing gum
and start the stalk and all the leaves
are green again.

Constance Hunting

Year-round

With what deceptive gradualness
the summer guests depart,
bearing the various trophies of their stay,
shells, dried kelp, a sea bird's skull,

leaving for our instruction shards of a season's
visit: sand on the stairs,
odd sneakers, a torn sweater, a child's ball,
and on the dressing table an unmailed letter.

One afternoon the last car disappears,
the hand raised in farewell flags, drops.
We linger a moment at the edge of lawn,
knowing that soon we must go in,

desert the view, diminish scene. Bring in the chairs
from the terrace, store the picnic things,
cover the boat. The house will need repairs—
look, that shutter flaps.

Only, the clock gnaws in the hall
like a mouse within the rind of yellow time.
Let us make tea, revive the art
of conversation; read; take naps.
A toothless sea mumbles at the crusts of the land.

Constance Hunting

The Perfectionist

with apologies to John Crowe Ransom

She certainly died, though not
of the general human
fever. Of chills
which proved mortal she died,
and a conflict of wills,
and the rigor of pride.
In her vacuum she abhorred
Nature. Nature finally scored.
Her refrain:
"Choose. Reject.
Discard. Maintain.
The stars are false,
they've moved again."
See now the tall
and adamantine brow.
Beneath the lids
closed by the unsought mercy
of the living, eyes must be
still stonied by denial. Strict-
boned hands cling to
a wreath long withered.
Therefore in pity at least
let us bring a winter
garland spiky with unforgiving
green, darkly articulate,
the colder the weather
grows more defiant, and more beautiful.

Constance Hunting

Coming Home

I leave my armor by the umbrella stand and enter.
    At the first word I think of stone
        walls, sea meadows, and the sweet
            fearful smiles of old ladies in streetcars.

Blood of my blood and bone of my bone
they sit and stare me down.
His hands with tender spots of age
spread like soft meat on either knee.
"The hollyhocks this year—the salt air
brightens them, y' know. (Had you forgotten?)
What d' you have out there—
linden, is it? Immigrant shrub."
Her fingers clasp each other in the lap
where once, unborn, I must have leapt
half symbol, half embarrassment.
"We were a little disappointed—" she begins,
with terrible timidity.
Love trembles in the proferred cup.

Then seedling, shifting, swelling,
sprouting, flourishing, brandishing, shaking-
shouting tree of pride, fruits pumice-
textured, clustered, shrunken,
color of never and despair—
                                        but after all,
what have they done to me, what crime
committed time on time in this small room?
And my own children, yet to be?
Splay-fingered, milky-mouthed, they will of course
love me, love me, love me.

Constance Hunting

At Mrs. R's

Breaking the surface of the long umbrageous room,
rising as from the foam of some dry Venus-sea,
exquisite out of the Aubusson, the tea table:

bearing its rosy wreath of cakes and marzipan,
crested with silver urn perched and craftily jointed
like some heraldic creature wrapt from myth
and set to brood on china (Limoges) eggs.

One looks in vain for a mosaic eye.

The diffident sun, a poor relation
bidden at four, limps in pale vestments,
borrowed, down the andante gloom
peopled with cabinets and manners;
takes refuge finally in ambiguities
of shaded glass shielding too-soft breath
of calculated bloom.

Here pity is no more possible than beauty.

Meanwhile the alternate Thursday connoisseur,
approaching with tainted smile the hooded chair,
notes once again how authentic and how rare
the narrow anachronistic foot
suspended in its pliant, pointed case
of dull bronze leather at the end of the relique-
thin leg of her who is curator and core
of this unique collection opened to a select et cetera.

They say she sometimes sucks a ruby like a plum.

Constance Hunting

Fever Nurse

I take it my real child is ill.
The worm works in the rose, and fever
glisters in tower windows.
Can my thorn draw her poison?

Extreme caution must be exercised.
I must exercise extreme caution.
My medicine is very powerful.
It has already killed several.

I stand at the foot of her white bed
and tell her of her pet toad
whom she has named Mortimer, after
a friend of the family. I say that Mortimer,

patient, self-effacing, utterly reliable,
waits for her under the laurel hedge.
Her eyes are so bright!
Outside, the rain falls like fat gray slugs.

Constance Hunting

Bird in Hand

The way the poet eats the hard-boiled egg
is this: he first chips delicately all round
the thin resistance of the shell of fact
which falls like flakes (if alabaster
melted so it would before
his beaming eye) as flicked
by his dactylic finger, to reveal
the gleaming nacreous shape
like a monstrous pearl—
he bites, good appetite, the simile in two
and sinks his teeth in muse's pollen,
golden, dusty, the real thing
that might once spring a phoenix to confound
the ovoid gape of his astonied stare.

Constance Hunting

Meadow Happening

My grandfather once saw a black-
snake in the act
of swallowing a frog.
Quick as lightning Grandfather
fetched the axe,
smote that snake like thunder.
The frog sprang out and sprang away
across the meadow—likely to start
a new religion. Grandfather said
you never saw a frog
leap so high!

Constance Hunting

A Dream of Heavenly Love and Redemption in the Wood

Damn her whose image on my nightly eyes
Rises unbidden by my daytime brain,
Damn her, the false nun gliding black on snow
Within the winter wood to find my places out.
No shudder of stricken leaf foretells
Her coming where I cower amid thorns,
But all the birds sit frozen on the boughs.
Tall as a tower comes she down the ride,
Her train of sable fancies in attendance close;
From a sly fold of her dark habit, lies
Hang like a rosary to be told, or little bells
To cast a different death, to tell a different hour.
Her snouted hounds of Grace and Mercy run beside,
Fawning and leaping on their lengths of chain,
And all the birds sit frozen on the boughs.
Nearer they come, the ladies twittering, but she
Stopping them of a sudden with a hand
Raised as in supplication or surmise—
Mass in the thicket, compound of blood and fear,
Signal of tiny beating in the air, the pulse of red
Betraying the human trespass of the wood.
The dogs know now. Loosed at her nod, they do not bark
But come on silent as the trees,
No pause, no check, no circling back, but straight
To quarry, that stain on black and white,
And silent spring and before any cry
Can struggle from the beating throat
Beneath them, silently devour.
The softest clapping as of snowflakes shaken from sleeves,
A smile as calm and faceless as the dark
Attend me on my waking into sleep,
And all the birds sit silent on the boughs.

Constance Hunting

Minute Observations

—The owl is the
only bird who
reminds me of
a cat: it is the eye
like a single agate
cut in two
by a frugal crafter

—Hear the crows'
black
barking in the wood

—Toad
like a hackberry leaf
under the mulberry tree

—It was not the fault
of the gnat
that he flew
onto my eyeball
as I
was gazing at
the Parthenon

—Down at the cove
of the seven sycamores
even the fish
are singing
because
the girl in the red dress
is coming

—Suddenly
the Chinese elm
sheds its dark
crown of birds

Constance Hunting

JARED CARTER

A Meeting

They say out there somewhere
There may be particles that get—
I don't know how—an anti-charge,
So that they're similar, and yet,
From different universes.
Should they collide, they disappear:
Annihilate each other.
And even those vast galaxies,
Which look like stars from here,
May be completely different.
So if they hit—that's it.
The firmament, they say,
Might be creating itself this way,
Or may be uncreating. They
Don't know that much about it yet. Here—
You want another cigarette?
Watch now, while we two lovers stand
Upon this little bridge where
We have met to say goodbye,
And look into the darkness:
This burning match is
Mirrored down there somewhere,
And we may try to estimate
The distance to the water's surface
By seeing how far that dim reflection
Is lost within the quiet flow.
I let it go: two tiny points of light
Draw toward each other—
There's no real rise or fall,
Only a meeting in the stream.

Jared Carter

A Drawing in the Tate Gallery:

"The Man Who Taught Blake Painting in His Dreams"

is still around somewhere . . . survived the smoke
and fires, the footsteps melting into stone,
the city dark within its haze of time;
endured, somehow, that face both epicene
and bold with innocence, though now withdrawn,
diminished, paled like some further star
to sit behind a stall near London Bridge;
yet lasted, since for painting lessons Blake
in turn taught him to sing, and in those dreams
they labored over angels, burning tigers,
bade their host prophetic spears cast down
and joyously to praise the Lamb—
. . . and found
themselves, still dreaming, charmed outside their dream.
Blake sailed away, for on each cobblestone
or casement glimmered visions of that realm,
and madly through the streets he danced and sang;
the man who taught him painting in his dreams
was left alone . . .
around him coiled the smoke
he watches through today, from park bench, pub,
or moving 'bus: listening for that strain
alone empowered to dream him back again.

Jared Carter

The Weaving

Her hands are braiding now her hair
Behind her back, while I
Admire such movement there:

Unerringly, sans watchful eye
Or mirror, she guides each strand
Into that simple ply;

Three quarters-finished now, but hands
In unexpected whim
Bring forward that soft band

And hesitate: her color dims,
Then blooms along the lifted
Beauty of her limbs;

Some prescience by which she's gifted
Suddenly divines,
Leaving the rest untwisted,

For now she weaves her arms to mine,
Completing with such care
This soft and ultimate
Entwine.

Jared Carter

Pompeii: Calco del Cane

"Cast of a chained dog (from the 'Casa di Vesonio Primo') who was caught by death while struggling with all his contracted sinews against the restricting chain (Plate LXIV, fig. 111)."

Pompeii, Instituto Poligrafico Dello Stato,
Liberia Dello Stato

Exploding still, after two thousand years,
He writhes within his pen of iron and glass,
While we observe that fiery moment pass
And marvel at such anguish, without fear.

The mule driver hunched beneath his cloak,
The woman turned face down, the others skulked
To cellars, leaving behind the dog to balk
Against a vanished chain that never broke.

Time passed. Then archeologists came
To pour impartiality into
These hollow testaments to sudden flame;

Toward casual eyes the dog's pale limbs
Now send a pulse so strong it passes through
Unfelt—as when a white star flares and dims.

Jared Carter

San Gimignano

"Six hundred sixty-three years earlier, the youthful ambassador Alighieri
arrived with an armed escort; and, in a painted room
Behind the balcony above, urged the magistrates of the Free Commune
to join with Firenze in the Tuscan League."

Except at high noon, the piazza is shaded by tall stone towers
of Guelph and Ghibelline; the pavement stones
Are footstep smooth, and laid in vast sweeping designs; the guidebook
compares them to a pattern of knives, or to the spines of fish.

"The monk Savanarola preached here, shortly before returning
to his native city; Gozzoli painted here; there are
Frescoes by Ghirlandaio in the Chapel of Santa Fina—
at whose death violets blossomed from the towers."

With black olives, bread, and Valpolicella, we sit now
in the cool shadows of the loggia, watching
Sunlight change the stones; the pigeons are nearly tame,
and willingly take scraps of bread from our fingers.

"Above, on the facade of the Palazzo del Popolo, are many armorial bearings,
beneath which the brothers Ardinghelli and their friend Bartoli,
Native Guelphs, were beheaded for plotting against the Ghibellines—
who later admitted there had been no conspiracy at all."

The American Express Tourist Special to Sienna bulls through the square;
suddenly a villager cries out, and kneels to retrieve
From beneath its treaded wheel, a pigeon, inexplicably caught:
a twitching heart down into the spinal curve of the stones.

"In 1507 the Florentine Secretary Machiavelli arrived
to train the townsmen in new arms and feats of patriotism;
They drilled in a place called the Fossi, near where
the old monastery of San Francesco stood."

In Tyrolean hats and wraparound sunglasses the tourists watch their driver
arguing with the townsman; he, brown of skin, in dusty clothes,
Gently lifts the enfeebled dove from the pavement,
its back broken, and holds it aloft—

"After the Medici, the French, the Austrians, after many years,
the towers of nobility began to fall; many were pulled down
By municipal order; only thirteen remain. Occasionally the wind,
rushing over their blank facades, makes a distant music."

—as though from the painted room behind the balcony above, someone
might yet be watching, waiting, sorting out the words
With which to address the empty piazza below, where now the sunlight,
passing noon, shifts the pattern of stone from spines to knives.

Jared Carter

The River

In the quiet valley
    Paw-paw
And persimmon bloom;
    Deer step
Momentarily from the gloom
    To water there
    By the Mississinewa

In the afternoons
    We go
Where the hawthorn flowers;
    And give
No thought to calm, inviolate hours
    We linger there
    By the Mississinewa

After Indian Summer
    Frost comes
And petals fade and blow;
    Deer leave
Not even footprints in the snow
    That falls there
    By the Mississinewa

Jared Carter

Rain in Late Autumn

Listening to the rain's penance
In the inevitable fall,
One hears beyond notes of sadness
Something not grief at all;

Coming and going, falling
And rising—all are parts
Joined like stone. Calling
Them more does not make of stones hearts.

Squeezed on all sides, what remains
Is not innocence, but what knows:
As when, lulled into darkness by rain,
One awakes at the changing to snow.

Jared Carter

Lullaby

". . . who admitted that she had killed her week-old daughter by feeding her barbiturates in a mixture of milk and honey . . . the baby was born . . . without arms and . . . deformed in other ways as well . . ."

New York *Times,* 12 October 1962

Before I lay thee down to sleep
Come linger on my breast
And hear thy mother's lullaby
To bring thee to thy rest.
    Receive thy portion unafraid,
    With lullaby, my little maid.

When thou wert safe within my womb,
From cares I sought relief;
Thy birth revealed that in this world
Escape still comes to grief.
    Receive thy portion unafraid,
    With lullaby, my little maid.

If poppy or if charms could cure
The sickness of this age
Apothecaries might give all
Yet still not check its rage.
    Receive thy portion unafraid,
    With lullaby, my little maid.

For meadows where all herds do graze
And hives wherein all bees
Store summer's flowers may soon be waste
And trees may end their leaves.
    Receive thy portion unafraid,
    With lullaby, my little maid.

Within this world thou need'st have hands
To weave thy husband's shroud,
And arms to hold thy children close
When death descends from clouds.
    Receive thy portion unafraid,
    With lullaby, my little maid.

The Book speaks of a promised land
Which some do journey toward,
Where milk and honey flow still pure
And plowshares bloom from swords.
    Receive thy portion unafraid,
    With lullaby, my little maid.

To guide thee toward that holy place
I have no power save this:
A lotos potion, sweet and warm,
As my last mother's kiss.
    Receive thy portion unafraid,
    With lullaby, my little maid.

Since Jesus came to give His life
For ours, upon the tree,
I'll risk my own to grant thee sleep
And spare thee misery.
    Receive thy portion unafraid,
    With lullaby, my little maid.

God made the world in seven days
And rested on the last;
And when thy mother's song is done
Thy seven days are past.
    Receive thy portion unafraid,
    With lullaby, my little maid.

Jared Carter

An Epitaph of Flowers

"Gravestones tell truth scarce forty years"
Sir Thomas Browne

Come, mistress, 'neath this hawthorn rest
And view this work we first began in jest,
But finished in a strange solemnity
That's lately rather silenced you and me.
What can I say to make you gay and merry?
Look out upon this ruined cemetery
And see how we have shaped it, put the stones
Back on the pedestals, and hoped the bones
Beneath would somehow match these monuments
So scattered by the seasons' elements;
For human hands have also desecrated
These tombs a hundred years have consecrated:
Teen-agers from the town in recent years
Have brought out here their blankets and their beers;
They knock down gravestones mightily, and after,
Lose all their present cares in present laughter.
And rumor has it there's a pimp in town
Who brings his whores out here—so on the ground
The happy customer gets his ten minutes
Without a care, beyond the city limits.
A thrill, I'd think, to buy a round-the-world
Upon a dirty army blanket, whirled
By some tongue's artificial stimulation
To think about one's own degeneration
And yet to muse upon the grandeur of
Perversion roused by some hard whore's unlove—
Superior far to lodging in that room
(One's round-the-world journey's end) the tomb.
You're not amused? But still, you helped to set
These stones upright, and deck with violet
And wild rose each weathered limestone face;
You wrote in fragile color where no trace

Of human legend stays, an epitaph
Of flowers.
Don't be morose, my dear, let's laugh,
And realize that those poor souls beneath
Rejoice in their re-ornamented heath!
Why yes, they're still down there all right—you see
The richness of this grass, so velvety
And green? A natural carpet, highly prized;
No wonder, for it's amply fertilized.
What do you mean, my little jokes are gruesome?
In all this place, we are the only twosome
Who know we're us: ours is a combination
More rare than all these stones' commemoration.
Just contemplate this yard of souls, who died
In willing separation from this side
Of paradise, in blest anticipation:
However parted from this life's temptations,
Still they were buried 'neath their proper stones
Which kept their names and histories for bones
To don again at that last trumpet blast.
And now the joke's on them, for stone won't last,
And pairs of graves and monuments are split
And parts re-shuffled—but that's not half of it:
For when the trumpet blows there'll be real
Bluffing 'mongst these wild cards in that big deal.

I see your eyes are fresh as flowers now—
Don't think about that showdown yet, but how
We two have staged our own apocalypse
With miniature omnisciency, in trips
Across this meadow lugging stones to place them
Where other forces struggled to erase them.
And just as we have sought to re-arrange
And form these scattered fragments on this grange,
Our afternoon of playtime may have mended
Some breaches which whole lifetimes had not ended.

For think upon these stones and bones, and see
There's not much difference; the memory
Which once held both together long since faded,
Till stones are equaled now with what they shaded.
These blank bare tablets hold a common trust
Of anonymity with buried dust,
And if someone should ask, "What mean these bones?"
The same dumb cry may echo from these stones.

Who knows? In standing them all up again
We may have bettered what did ne'er begin,
And joined at last some loyal old-maid teacher
(Who pined in silence forty years)
with her fair preacher.
Some bachelor, famed for his timidity,
We may have put in close proximity
Next to the village tart—who gives a sigh
That she's at last escaped the haughty eye
Which glared at her for ninety years in stone,
Marking the grave of pious Deacon Jones.
That big slab over there, now in the corner:
It may have been some oaf's who, without honor
(Save for a notice on society's page,
"A marriage reaches fifty years of age . . . ")
Entombed his wife in years of living sadness.
And now her stone, in unexpected gladness,
Is rolled next to the monument of one,
Her childhood sweetheart, fallen at Bull Run.
Enough of this Spoon River speculation!
We cannot know the joy or tribulation
Of those who linger here; but certainly
Our deeds may share this life, for them to see.
For no deciphering of ruined letter
Can spell the secrets which such ruins fetter;
Perpetuation of each epitaph
Depends on those like us, who, with a laugh,
Admit the heart's dread—that *our* legends be
No more, no less, than such proud fantasy—

And yet with love and care will re-create
A flowered semblance of that former state.

You're smiling now, but save your energy,
My love, for we have one last fealty
Remaining, one by which we'll try to pay
True homage to these honest tombs: a way,
A simple ritual which all have acted
Who're buried here, or later were attracted.
Whether they said the rites for selfish gain
Or altruistic love, it's all the same
To those below—only the elevation
Of bone within the flesh can bring elation
To their dust. And whether by this we'll chasten
Their spinning souls for heaven, or rather hasten
Our own to hell's beyond my speculation:
For I speak of a different immolation.

Come, with your charms now raise *this* monument,
And deck it with your last flower's ornament;
Its momentary resting-place will be
A lasting pledge to that felicity
By which gay tombs, though robbed, sustain no harm.
My archeologist! whose knowing arm
Restores the fallen edifice to glory!
Now learn the grandeur of this ancient story:
Against mute temple walls the tissue's pressed
As soft as petals which these graves have dressed;
And by such careful tracing all this hour,
We two into our epitaph will flower.

Jared Carter

Cardinal Bellarmine Recalls an Evening in February of 1616

Before the last, I dined with him five times,
And every evening's conversation seemed
To free us of the day's antipathies.
A kindly man, I thought, for when we talked
Before the fire, he steered away from hints
Of how he thought the moon looked through his glass,
Or how some demon had deranged his sight
Each time he dared to gaze upon the sun's
Incomparably smooth sphere. Kindly, yes,
But also mad; quite evidently so.
A fool's task, to journey all that way
In hope of gaining dispensation which
Would let him crack the heavens like a nut,
Yet never ask himself just why the Pope
Was too involved to grant him audience.
That was my work; likewise I kept the Pope
From summoning him—another irksome task.

But ah! those evenings, we conversed like friends
From youth: of mutual acquaintances
And how they fared, of masques and manuscripts,
The Turkish problem, higher mathematics—
For which I shared his love—and arguments
Begun at eight sometimes went on past one.
So passed those evening visits, while by day
The Qualifiers of the Holy See
His blasphemous suggestions read. I helped
To plan those secret sessions, was among
The first to offer thanks to Mary Queen
For word of their decision. Quickly written
Out and then bound very handsomely—
Grey vellum flecked with gold, I think—I took
It to the chamber where we were to dine
A final time that night.

Of course he knew;
Things have a way of leaking out like that,
And in Rome's eye, I guess, he stood condemned,
Disgraced. Except the Pope, troubled by spells
Of gout that winter long, had failed to hear
And still was asking for him now and then.
After the pheasant, and a dry white wine
Brought from my chateau near Chablis, I told
The servants to retire until I called.
Bearing a silver plate of Donatello's—
Laden with pale green figs and other sweets
Arrived from Macedon—we slowly took
Our chairs before the porphyry fireplace.
I did not think that he would say straight off,
"My trunks and bags are packed, and in two days
"I leave . . . " oh no, for he was much too sly;
In all those weeks before, he'd argued till
My brain seemed wired and looped and doubled back
With all his treacherous cycles, epicycles,
Arcs and sines, and thus I knew he'd not
Admit he knew. We chatted for a while,
Though all this time the proclamation lay
Conspicuous upon a special table
Less than three feet away.

"Let us suppose,"
He said eventually, in tone of voice
Resembling more our afternoons than nights,
And with a curious coughing—rather, clearing
Of his throat, which signaled serious talk—
"Let us suppose we've taken ship, and deep
"Within the hold, where neither light of day
"Nor ravenous cry of gulls nor murmuring waves
"Can penetrate. For some time now we two
"Have sailed, but still the steady temperate winds
"And rowers' even strokes propel us so
"That to our sense we might be yet on land.

"Suppose then you and I, old shipmates true,
"Awake some night, and, still half-drugged by sleep,
"Forget our voyage, neglect beneath our feet
"The very pitchy planks, inquire instead
"Where we may be? We light a smallish taper,
"Sit us down to have this problem out.
"The candle flame burns steadier than a widow's
"Heart for love—excuse, your Excellency—
"And this convinces you we're still on land.
"By chance I have with me a deft lodestone
"Fetched by old Marco Polo from Cathay,
"And since the ship is moving very fast,
"By reading from this needled dial an hour
"Or two apart, I plot the diagrams
"Which indicate we're changing latitude.
"You disagree; I let you check the stone:
"See how it draws the bits of metal laid
"Within your heavy rings, your loops of beads?
"A lodestone, and no doubt about it; you
"Observe as each additional reading shows
"We're traveling west, and plainly not on land
"But far at sea. Then how, your Excellency,
"Do you defend your senses five from what
"They cannot grasp but science proves? Cast out
"That lodestone, and we're lost, even on land;
"Or would you grudgingly admit we float,
"But since you feel no motion, rather claim
"The sea moves under us while we stand still?"
For such tirade from lesser man, I think,
I would have cut the evening short, and said
Quite curtly, "Jesus in His mercy guides
"My way." But mark you, how this Galileo
Stood upright, glaring so strangely now—
A basilisk! "Say instead," I breathed,
While looking deep into his hard grey eyes,
"There are more miracles in heaven and earth
"Than mortals such as we may ever know."

He waxed quite volatile, though not at me—
Rather an inward bursting, choleric
And cruel, yet still contained within himself:
Control so great to match that of the whale,
That stoic fish who swallowed Jonah whole
(With several barrels of ocean, plus the brine
Which Jonah wept while raging down inside.)
I thought it best to let him seethe, to mark
His every move, lest he prove dangerous
To me or even to himself. This was
His humour, then; the proclamation lay
Unmentioned on the table, contents known
But unconsidered now, for he had set
The parable of all we could not grant.
I watched him struggle, then, as from great depths
A pearl fisher bursts to gasp and heave
The lighter element into his lungs
Until he rests serene upon the waves.
He walked around the room three times, tapped hard
Against a cornice, stood full minute long
Before a small Sassetta frame—Saint
Anthony's Temptation, I believe—
Ah yes, it was, and quite a favorite
Of mine. Back at my side, he seized a fig,
Bit it in two, ate half, and spit the other
In the fire. "So!" addressing self
More than your Uncle Bellarmine, it seemed,
And with a single motion more, strode
Straightway out the door, and thence on back
To Vallombrosa.

Years ago that was,
And since that time, he's little heard, they say.
The Church, as always, steers the straightest course,
Unbuffeted by devilish schemes like his.
The sun and all that heaven contains go round
This gloriously appointed earth, my sons.

Look out, see for yourself. Had Galileo
Had his way, and laid his circles 'fore
That silly Pope, who knows what heresies
Might spread dissension through our schools now?
It matters not that I deceived one man
Nor even that I duped the Pope (small task).
Of choice, with truth; but of necessity,
Then even with lies, thus must we ever strive
To keep our law, our Church, our universe
Firmly in place.

Now go, my sons, I've talked
Too much this afternoon, and rambled far
Too long on minor matters. Giovanni,
Evening star and flower of my old age,
Will'st stay with me a while? Ah, that's a boy,
Yes here, beside me close upon the bed.
What would you have? A clock? Your uncle sick
These several days, and you come asking gifts?
What make of clock would do—an hourglass,
Perhaps, or sundial for your mother's house?
Or a big clock, one that's wound, and ticks
All day and night, its pendulum as bright
And ponderous as any general's sword?
You shall have clocks someday, my son, with dials
Of amethyst and ruby, pendulums
Of gold. How strange—in telling of that time
With Galileo, I remember now
A detail I forgot to tell your brothers,
The mystery of that single move he made
Before he left me sitting by the fire—
A fire that seemed to dwindle all at once.

Well, a clock stood next the western wall
Between two matching paintings by Carrucci—
Allegories, I recall, The Sack
Of Troy displayed in one, the other Jove,
Perhaps Prometheus, it slips my mind—
He stepped between those frames and thrust his hand

Into the open clockwork, clutching hard
The massive pendulum, which gave a groan
And then was still. That was the last I saw
Him do.

Alone, I sat till morn, watching
The fire softly falling to ashes, thinking
How I had given defense for all I love,
Remaining motionless within that room
More stilled than any place imaginable—
Until dawn flared upon Saint Peter's dome,
That light awakening me from troubled dreams.

Jared Carter

DAVID F. GLADISH

Just Once a Wave

Zeus was smart, all right. I
Appreciate, I think, the nuances
Of the bull, the swan, the golden
    Shower of rain, but

Why did the father of all wisdom
Not check with Old Proteus how
To be water, and come in
    Just once a wave?

Hot rain can kiss a lot of
Little times, warmer than feathers tickle,
And a bull—well, . . . But a warm kiss
    Of a wave is full length.

I'd be the sun, first, and
Shine on you a morning
On the sand, next, air to move,
    Cool, over those veins, and

When the time came, on the tide I'd
Crest in, curl-sucking you under,
Roll you, dance boiling fingers
    On your raw me

Until I set you, gently, on the
Sand (half-quick), and slid away
Often to lap back as one final
    Kiss full length.

David F. Gladish

A Paradigm

I startled her. Suddenly
I awoke, fairly before
The soft knock dropped from the panel
Of my door and my mother's dry voice
Drove gently through black, "It's all over,"
Startled her because of vigor that was young,
Uncluttered, instant, and alive,
And her husband was no more:
No more, my father.

Nothing came unstuck at once.
No revelation came.
There was a dry-eyed night like any other,
Not more hopeless, lonesome,
Not more terrible
Just cold,
For my shrinking soul
Withdrew to the timeless, senseless present,
As his soul must have brooded, on its own.

II

Tears came ten years, twelve years later,
For he died again:
Died when I found not priest nor law
Nor friend, nor soul companion,
No, not a nerve or brain-cell
That could tell, in this washing
Water of a world,
What thing if done were well.
Then tears came, and he died.
Tears and a song came, and he died.
A childhood song came back.
After the tumult came a still, small voice.

III

Again I lost my father
When I met an old man
And he said, "You've got his hair."
I asked him what my dad was like.
"I borrowed his coat once
To shoot ducks. That was the year I got my shotgun,
Not the first one, but . . . .
Yup, you've got his hair.
Well, well he's dead . . . .
I've still got the shotgun . . . ."

A man has got as many lives as a cat.
My father was a good man.
He could look out for himself,
But he died the other night at the show.
Soldier of fortune, lumberjack, airman,
Also gentleman. Banker and husband
By the time I was his son.
He died when the hero
Knocked down the villain
And a voice
Two rows back
Scoffed, "Oh, Clark, that's all you know."

IV

Alone. At last alone my father rose that black night
Long ago, from a world of form
Where the man learned: father,
Husband, banker, gentleman,
Airman, lumberjack,
Child, and before that some vague numbness.

In the nest and world of the unborn,
Form has bound a foetus
To a form, and left.

I, too, left a world.
That world that coddled me
Knew but relief, for the ripe fruit
Strains the bough.

Strange if an absent nothing bent
With a warm breath and a resounding voice,
And a firm hand shook the firmament,
And a naked babe lay rocked
In a strong, knuckled, curl of palm.
Strange if a numb sense opened at one tiny point
Or a babe grew
Till a vague gigantic motion full of sound
Spoke, and it seemed a word.

Only birth is born, but the future
Groans, big with abortive death.

V

At a knock I woke, and a living voice
Hung on the livid atmosphere of death.
That night we parted, Father and I.
Voices from a numb surrounding
Whispered, "Come," and oblivion filled us each
With a new world.

David F. Gladish

If Only

If only you
Were night sky
And I a whole
Hour's supply of
Fireworks.

David F. Gladish

Death Is Dreadful

"Death does make us wise, when by his coming our Affairs are past." Sir William D'Avenant.

Death is dreadful, loathing, shocking.
    Death is frank
    As a shank
In a wrinkled, rotten stocking.

Death is candid as a musty
    Heap of junk
    In a trunk,
Put away to keep, and dusty.

Like a thirty-dollar hat
    On the neat
    Leather seat
Of an auto with a flat,

Or a bleak suburban lot,
    After all
    In the fall
When the vegetable rot

Only testifies derision
    Of the sweat
    That you let
For your cultivated vision,

Death chuckles at the labor
    We expend
    To pretend . . .
Death does make us wiser, neighbor,
    In the end.

David F. Gladish

Reflections in a Pool

The bathers were a pretty average lot:
Saggy as though perhaps unpressed or made
Wrong in the first place, overused and not
Laundered properly, allowed to fade.

Long legs uncertainly supported great
Abdomens. Dauntless thighs, and chins a bit
Grand were matched with bony chests, and fate
Might well have swapped around and made things fit.

One couple in the shallow end were hugging
Two half-drowned babies bleating like two lambs.
Some strutted from the shower door tugging
Tight, shimmering tricot over flabby hams.

A youth, with maiden shoulders, had a maid
With youthful buttocks like a boy's. He'd caught her,
And they were half in love and half afraid.
And Man moved on the faces of the water.

David F. Gladish

Proteus

Youth I've got you! Now, Old Man, you hate to tell
the truth, don't you. You twist and struggle. Well,
you devil you, you god, you father . . . Now
is it a chalky teacher, is it? How
about a poet, say, or friend, or bride,
or minister . . .? No sooner said than tried,
and look what use it was, you fop—you phony.
Strike any pose you like, it's all baloney
while my good grip will pinch until you're through
and have to tell me something really true.

Man You've got me? I've got you, you little snip.
Look at you duck your head and try to slip
between my legs, you frightened little rabbit.
Why not a snake, or would you take the habit,
and then there'd be a dozen years of, oh,
logic and fallacies. . . . What matter, though?
If time is what it takes, well, I can wait
and watch amused whatever shape of hate,
chameleon, or pink unvarnished ruth
you want to choose . . . or love. And that's the truth!

David F. Gladish

On Beginning a Reading of *Paradise Lost*

Steer on, O Palinurus of the soul,
To that first painful sense of severed strength—
Bone-chilling hardship and false hope the toll—
Till from the dark the star descends at length.
Steer on. This is a voyage that will end
When, like Ulysses, every favorite fault
Unlocked, and vanished every noble friend,
I wash up naked but for a crust of salt.
Steer on through borrowed Eden, that the scent
Of very Wisdom sculpted as a world
May fill my nostrils, and my thrilling ears
The harmony of Life divinely lent.
Then, out of Paradise mercif'ly hurled,
Steer on to Paradise through sweat and tears.

David F. Gladish

Curiosity

Needle-sharp hooks, a fog of shaggy hair
Off-white like a tobacco-stained mustache
In places and as long almost against
The padded paws as on the fuzzy ears—
It was a polar bear reared dizzily
And tall, grinning and massive there and silent
Within the frozen dustless stillness of
His glass case. And the man before him,
At parade rest nearly, had woven through
The glass a binding web-work made of pure
And academic curiosity.
The bulbous nose that poked between the full
Red beard and wire-rimmed spectacles reflected
That black muzzle (the only spot close-cropped):
Creature with creature intimate, the one
Two-thirds as tall, lips pursed and eyes asquint,
The other fierce raw integrated power.
Three children gathered clutching luncheon sacks
And dimes, their well-made blouses out and hats
Awry, and open-mouthed, to watch the beard.

David F. Gladish

Red

None of it was for me,
but I stole some of it, because
there she stood,
With her yellow skirt
quivering on her authoritative
thighs, and her eyes
almost as hungry as the ones
in *my* head.

When she leant on the Juke,
bent ankle twined with hip's
rhythm, spike heel ground me
right in the groin, and

A sense of the sheer art
parted the zing and the
head-strings in me till I
sniffed where the heat aimed—
not at me;

At a slob with a spare
tire big in back as the one
in front, with a fat
ear lobe and all, and I

Can't help thinking
red is too bowl-me-over
hot to be fired
at a green fly
lightly from a
blunderbuss.

David F. Gladish

Lavov

What arcane dark
Animal economy
Connected woman-
Kind and creatures?

Stuck in the boondock
Keeping a pretty
Widow's household,
Once I wondered.

Two hens chuckled
Upstairs; downstairs
Hatching ducklings,
Dank in the seeping
Cellar, quickened.

This house smelled of
Musty mammals:
Red hound, black dog,
Coon-dog, lap-dog,
House dogs—indolent,
Livingroom-cluttering
Kennel club catalogue—
Cat, alive inside,
Big b' the fireside,
Every last dead-asleep one
Gone Jordanside.

Childhood breathed
Aloft all softly,
Claw-sore cheek where
Cat alive gored her
Under the tablecloth,
Knit with intricate
Blood-clot flesh knots.

Awful life all
Absent, ancient and
Tender slumber
Turned articulate:
"All our job is
Breath and life-blood,
Her reward but
Our vitality."

This arcane dark
Animal apology,
Heart-beat mystery
Drowsed about me.

David F. Gladish

The Shore

Late August. In the cold dawn, not
a footprint insults the swept order of
the windy, inland beach, but a man is there;
the chafing palms rub
a little heat into the paper-cold skin.
Forty, alert, a little bent,
he puts a heel down off the duck-board walk
that swims in sand below the foot of wooden
stairs, below the bluff. The bare, cold foot
grates on the dry, cold sand. Cold sand here,
for the sun is still behind high green
red-oak, bass, and hemlock trees above them all—
Man, Shade, and Sand.

A hand-spring in a burst
of youth.
He shuffles, for the low,
assertive whistle that the sand can make,
and at a beach-long windrow of a high-water mark,
picks out a way through sharp things dried or slimy—
dead fish fins, foamy slag, a board with licks
of tin and green-black snot and greenbacked snails.

Then, to the waves still blown enough to curl
in green and momentary shells that flop
like tackled, shoulder-padded shoulders. He wades
to the knees, hitching up his ancient ducks.
The gasping man absorbs the wind; water
by floods soaks the rolls of the trousers, sand
sucks his feet up and he is a moment
fit, like fish and slimy flotsam, to belong
euphoric in the weather. And the wind
sings harsh; on the hard shore the deep drums.

Driftwood windrow, sand, a living man—
all fit to one green plain of beach and lake-top.

2.

Wind is wrenching what is dry enough
and whipping little puffs, where down the swept
face and shell of one clean dune a girl
flies, with expansive, bare-foot step for the lake-side.
Wind laying back her loose hair, down
she runs from the bluff and shades. The laughing lips,
the bow brows, and the chin have found a gentle
joke of life. The deep blue eyes are silent.

This is a Girl that loves a Boy
(and he's a Boy with a heart of gold
a Boy with a raw-boned, robust body,
braving the thin-lipped world of just-so,
snug in the hug of a clear blue vision
three sheets full with sheer solutions).

Girl and Man, now they squat beside
last night's beach fire, on the cold sand.
But see, where the boy comes,
loping side-wise, big with youthful
flexibility, gracefully loose-hung,
rhythmic.

Now it's a little world of three on the beach—
The Boy, the Man, the Girl—and the drab sand
by the green sea flows to a sickle point
far off, where electric blue above and green
below unite, where beach and bluff, colorless,
mingle in a single simple mist.

Three pair of eyes in turn. The weather in
a few small words. The man's eyes drift to the sickle
point and contemplate. The boy is searching
for a skipping-stone. She's searching him.
A sinewy, raw-boned boy, nervous and serious,
mysterious for the girl, and for himself.

On the shore stand the three.
On the stair, they laugh, to see
a little bare-foot three-year-old
double-stepping on the grown-up steps,
shedding sweaters as he goes,
calling, "Daddy," to the man,
Who sweeps him in a strong arm, and they two run
to the hard sand, to dig (the little knees
and back an exact anlage of the big) the summer's
finest castle "for the girl."

"That makes
two to dig and two to give directions":
Raw-bones.

And the girl: "Make me a fine castle,
Little Man . . . Your mother dressed you warm
when you left your cozy cabin."

"Heavy
clothing, healthy boy," says the man.

As the castle grows and the sun grows hot
and the child gets off his little shirt
and the girl hugs her legs, and her toes scoop sand,
and the boy stoops and flings skipping-stones—
stoops and flings—and the gulls above on the wind
beat up, or swing down the rushing, flowing,
overflowing air, suddenly there's
another on the shore,
with a stick: the Playful Friend
who won't grow up forever.
Full of oats, and ready,
burly and squat, and square;
fair, and balding early;
smug, and adolescent
balanced; all of a piece;
with a stick to taunt with.

He greets the boy with a playful poke,
a poke that digs in ribs and shoulders—
accidental, irrepressible,
insignificant, overwhelming.

"Hi (poke) friend (poke)
(poke-poke-jab-poke).
Getten any? (jab-poke-*poke*)."

Catch it, Raw-bones. Upsy-daisy.
Butt-for-teacups, under water.
Raw-bones comes up dripping wet.
That's enough. He's met his match.
Seething, breathing injured anger,
off he stalks, but she beside him.

The child says, "Daddy, why can't *I* go swimming?"

The Child, the Man. And now the Permanent Youth
(the Joke, the Stick, the Quickness of a Beast)
fresh from the service, rough and hearty, never

a moment older, more than the man, a long sight,
master of his every least faculty.
Rough and Tumble, with a yen to measure.

A short, sandy scuffle, and the man can't
find the snap to whip the brash pup.
The child straddles the heap, the hero, bravely
bouncing on the victor of his dad.

3.

Evening and the cold sand is black
as the deep, till the eye takes in the starlit frill
of surf. Man and Girl and once again
The raw-boned boy, new-bruised and battered,
better "'Cause I found him somewhere
minus stick. He left his guard down!"
Rubbing raw-boned jaw: "I showed him."

And then the girl's seaward gaze snaps
to the man, and "Tell me, wise one,
when do men grow up?"

"Never, of course," he poses.
"But youth is out-bound on a spring day: invited,
beckoned, challenged every way, and every
way's a possibility. Unlimited
choice. Youth therefor tries them all (or youth
that's worth a damn does) until the day wanes,
and home is in only one direction . . ." But
the Girl and Raw-Boned Boy are gone.

4.

Wind sings no longer, and no more
does the sting of blown sand prick the calf.
A day has changed all that, and the waves
lap gently, far apart, in a dead calm lake.
The Milky Way is immediate in the deep
blue cold above the air, and the tight,
righteous mechanism far out there

turns the deliberate immensity of earth
Enough for a sliver moon to peep through high
Red-oak, bass, and hemlock; turns and turns,
And, motionless, the man, alone, turns on it,
still and fitting and a bit of all of it.

David F. Gladish

Plains

So that the green land, supine,
Black underneath and rich as the night landscape
Might not virgin into ashes someone
Came to make tracks and tracings.

Down to work. Athwart the sight
A cross-hatch—that was it:
Walls beyond walls of longitude
To show where the concrete lines had got to go.

That keeps the outside out
In case you look across the vacant lot
Or distance fix the naked eye
Too deep.

And keeps the river in the rainy street
Rippling past at a safe distance
Beyond the sidewalk,
Beyond the porch railing,
Beyond the storm window and the window,
And far beyond the horn-rimmed spectacles.

David F. Gladish

RAY MIZER

Confessions of a Forgetful Man

I have never once in all my life, not once,
Known hunger as a madness in the blood,
Nor long, except by choice, been shelterless;
Have not lived long with violence at flood,
Nor wrestled no holds barred with daily pain.
What I do suffer is amnesia . . .
Or possibly a touch of anesthesia.
I swear that I will not forget again.

Those swarms that settle on the garbage dump
To feed are human. Should my vow be vain,
I know not how, much longer, to sustain
The binding tie. How know man in the lump
As man? Those wretched howling multitudes
Breeding like flies and like flies perishing—
Tell me you see in these similitudes.
What! In these festering hordes? The image of God?
India, Hong Kong, China, Congo, South America?
The sardine squares of Europe's packing crates?

Stand back a bit. Get distance. These are men?
Come back. There is a nearer reckoning
On streets of home, where all the feet are shod,
Accents familiar.
Do I dispossess
The mob? Reject, disclaim fraternity?
Let me be honest now. Say: If I could,
I would reject the bond, deny the tie.
For why?
For I abhor, abominate
Stupidity and filth and cruelty;
I am intolerant of intolerance;
Fanatically resist fanatics; yes,
Hate haters and (one may as well confess)

Prefer some ignorance of the ignorant.
Well, then. Almost I do forget myself.

I swear that I will not forget again.

Ray Mizer

Garden Hints

I.

From where I lay in the cunning grass
Pillars of lifting tulips propped the sky:
Bright green the shafts, their pedestals probing earth;
Intensely bright the capitals
Holding a frieze of cloud,
An architrave of blue.
But while I slept a walloping wind arose
And all those glittering columns buck-
    led and swa
yed. And then in one outrageous roar
The vault collapsed,
    the dome of heaven
fell
And only the grass was glad.

II.

What is that fat green caterpillar doing
Dawdling on my dahlias?
Damn his limp pistachio heart!
That goes for the hinged brown hopper of the grass
Who bypassed grass,
Whirring to settle on a glad.
They eat. And having eaten, eat again,
Voraciously, leaving me with a stem.
What does this footed belly know of flowers,
Or this winged jaw of fragile blossomings?

Sometimes at dusk, when light is right for viewing,
I see our gardens marked for sacrifice:
From horizon to horizon drooling hordes,
Insatiate armadas settling in.
The rumbling of their bellies fills the air:
Louder than insects,
More basic than blossoms.

III.

The bright jay railed from the poplar.
Unseen, but seeing;
Taunting the stalking cat and me,
Shrilling defiance.
    So far beneath him:
    A cat with murder in his mind
    For whom wings carried meals alone,
    And I, illiterate in arts of flight,
    But well versed in derisive screech
    Of hunted to balked hunter.
I could not, in good conscience,
Translate that jay's diatribe;
Still less repeat for tender ears
The cat's thoughts when
Cat-tired with being cursed,
He sensed I voted for the raucous blue,
Those bright unspeakable wings,
And turned on me a parting look
Venomous as blind instinct alone
Could hope to muster.

IV.

Consider this lowly onion here
(Or, if your taste is delicate,
Its more aesthetic cousins).
Each knows the worth of many skins
Each quite complete, each shaped to each;
Stripped one by one, layer by layer,
Eroded by frictions that come with time,

It rests complete,
Down to the very heart of the matter.

V.

How could a thing with winter blood
Be so summer as a toad?

VI.

Ubiquitous, this sprawling wench,
This trespasser with the golden tresses.
She is seductive in her salad days,
And gay in her wine-bearing youth;
But her teeth are the teeth of the lion,
And her milk curdles fast in the vein.
Her dancing head weaves golden dreams
But there is hollowness beneath;
And when her time is come,
She raises a fake halo round her head
And throws her children on the mercy of the wind.

VII.

Hunkered under the dahlia bush
Haloed in a whirling sunburst of bloom,
This baggy, blinking bloat of a toad
Surveys the blazing autumn casually.
Indifferent alike to red and gold,
His hop is tentative and restrained,
Essays no leap into a rarer air;
This clod beneath the gay stalked sun
Burns with so low a flame
As scarcely to notice when the sun goes out
And limply blackened, prostrate slumps to clay.
In dank adobe slumber he will hibernate
Until another sun restore the day.
Such chary, calculated preservation
Almost lends fillip to extinction.

VIII.

The brave snail summoned all his strength,
Called his coiled courage up, and winced.

IX.

Look(!) Just one drop of oil
On this lackluster pool here
And rainbows swirl riot:
Lucullan lubricity.

X.

That winged ruby flash from the lilac bush
Shattered hyperboles clean into April.

XI.

Who could have forseen
    the earthworm's turning
        in such a pink frenzy
            across white stones.

XII.

"What bitter spite and enmity were here
To so burlesque creation's paragon?
Time scratched those gullies in her cheeks
And hung the Doppelganger on her chin;
Time sagged the bouncy firmness of those breasts;
Time bulged the ankles, cracked the voice,
And turned to rolling hills her fertile plains."

A poet's fancy in a hackneyed style.
And Housman said it better long ago.
Let it alone. Besides, it's dubious doctrine.
We do not mourn that grain matures in husk,
Bewail the full blown rose,
Nor curse that summer follows vernal promises.
Who would have apples always green?
Or buds forever buds, or spring forever spring?

I might. This talk of ripening wine and grain,
Plump fruit and open flowers does us no good.
I will sit here awhile, vituperating time
That has no sense of knowing when to stop:
That must turn perfect apples to brown mush,
Make of these perfect blossoms green manure,
And of a perfect woman something very like a jest.

XIII.

That conflagration rooted in blackness
With green smoke rising
Is my dahlia bed.

XIV.

It's those same damn buzz-saw locusts again!
Chewing up summer with pigiron jaws.

XV.

Over there
where the row suddenly
stops being tulip
and becomes daffodil
for a clump space
then turns tulip again,
Any damn fool can see
something is right.
That bright daffodil
true to some bulbous
impulse or design
hit on the notion
of just being daffodil
same as per always
and to hell with trying
to be a tulip.

XVI.

They had been here all winter, the cedar waxwings.
We often saw them busy in the junipers,
Crests perky as a colt's ears,
Sociably sharing the berries between them.
They wore a thief's mask of black,
But they weren't thieving;
The yellow-tipped tails bobbed in greeting.
They were fearless. What should they fear?
Oh, he was beautiful, but so was she.
They had mastered the arts of flight,
Knew all their enemies, were free to come and go;
Knew where food was, and shelter. They were a pair.
They had survived the winter's bitter worst;
Soon now would be time for nesting.
But today
They came in a great joyous swoop—both, both,
From the tip of the highest maple they came,
Diving in sheer springtime gladness, it seemed,
Into the bright pool of air they trusted to sustain.
But crystal air turned suddenly to glass:
Their taut brown sleekness crumpled instantly.
A broken spring: wings slacken, and from parted beaks
Song welling in a crimson froth, and eyes gone dim
Uncomprehending stare
At strange new springs beyond this instant night.

XVII.

Have you a real toad there?
In an imaginary garden?
Good. That is poetry.

Ray Mizer

Poets, Readers, Critics

I.

This balding, bad, bay-windowed boy
With pinkly pudgy hands and eyes that summon sleep—
This is a poet?!
Could that bright needle wit
Stick in this pin-cushion?
This? With all the glitter and glow
Of puffballs in the smog?
This outsize troll, by Bagstock out of Grendel's dam?
This bacchant Barbarossa?
Even so.

The lyric muse no doubt
Admits strange fellows to her bed.
Do not on this account deny the issue.
Poets are to be heard, not seen.
Pure poetry may be an essence, it's true,
But the basal ambergris
Grows not in leaping rainbow trout
Or fighting muskellunge,
But in abdominal despair
Among sick whales.

II.

I too would be beatific,
    making my coffee strong and syntax weak,
    always making the scene, albeit fuzzily.
When I am hooked, bepadded, and hirsute,
Besandalled and beset,
Then I would beatest be, O,
    excruciatingly Zen then
    even to existentialist Endsville;
Knowing all counsel blather and blah
I could contemplate like crazy

From navel to nullity, starting from scratch. Only
Don't wait up for me, dad.
Like, hell, this may take light years.

III.

I watch a spider spread his nets
With calculating artistry;
Then, smug within his silken sets,
Invite the critics in to tea.

With buzzing and judicial glance
The critics come. Quick as a wink
The play begins with frantic dance;
The curtain falls before they think.

Fishing is good. His play succeeds;
And living on his art, he dines.
He has fulfilled his inmost needs
With delicate yet gripping lines.

IV.

Bird found a poem in a bush
Where wind had published on a thorn
The latest leaf cast on the air
To lift toward fame or curl with scorn;

Approaching brightly twig by twig,
Inspecting with a critic's eye
From every angle as to what,
And how, and maybe why,

Then grasping it as birdfolk may,
Satisfied with heft and scope,
Flew off with it to line a nest
That hymned his own perennial hope.

V.

True, love, you have a way with words.
Away with words! I would have you,
Both subject and object,
With linking verb (subjective complement!)
In happy case and all sweet syntax be,
In perfect agreement,
That pure infinitive,
The subject understood.

You I would have,
Demonstrative if possible,
And possessive; intensive you,
So substantive, so causative.
O fair conjunction this,
The gender right past doubt;
O most emphatic conjugation!
Unmodified,
absolute,
beyond comparison.

VI.

The fierce-tempered little gent
With the delicate nose and chin
Is Mr. Aspic.
Formerly geared to Appreciate
(holding the fragile fragrance gently,
like a dear rose blown too full),
He has got, of late, the critical bug.
And he will, By God, play God.
Thus vowing that they shall not pass
With hackles rising risibly,
He daintily grasps the nether mane
To insert a cocklebur or twain
Beneath the proudly galloping tale
Of every prancing Pegasus.

VII.

Hamleting through Denmark,
Or byroning through Spain,
Intense young men ginsbergly seek
The golden ghost in vain;
Then in autumnal ennui,
Jet home on jaundiced wing
To Bagdad-on-the-Hudson
For a little dylaning.

VIII.

Real poetry—what I call real—
Is sharp. It will not serve to sleep on,
Nor to swallow. If it's real,
It cuts the living daylight into you
Or does a neat lobotomy.
It rides a clean keen edge between two falls
And either one is fatal.
Then too, real poetry has heat:
You reel shock shriven from that salient sun.
    Not like the stuff that you and I abhor,
    So dull it wouldn't cut soft soap
    So aromatically dead when hugely read.

Ray Mizer

Emancipator

And now, with slow decay of shapes, day ends.
The dark releases much reality;
These crusted facts and concrete figures doze.
There is no magic in a hard legality.

Day flows in lava tides out of sun's crater,
Inundates garden, tenement, and tower,
The watchman leaning sleepward by his shack,
And a statue of Warren Gamaliel Harding.
Fixing them adamant, moulded relentless in light.

Solvent of darkness looses, lets them go;
Erases angles, softens hard detail.
We come to something deeper than the fact,
More livable than concrete:
The misty boulevard,
The feathery tower,
The fragile web of bridge,
The something that the naked night sets free.

Ray Mizer

Guest of Honor

She sat emphatically alone
 in the honored place
 in the foremost pew;
Her crown a brown straw bonnet
 and around the crumbling brim
 a huddle of cherries, chipped,
 their whiteness showing through.
And later, after the unctuous eulogy,
 after the stranger's measured praise,
 they came to proffer aid,
 she shrugged them off.
Erect, with one hand resting lightly on the box
 she walked the outward walk alone;
And later still,
 on grass too green for winter,
 the bonnet at her breast,
 she plucked the cherries absently
 and tossed them one by one away.

Ray Mizer

Hover

We lure night down, recurrently,
To cover with jet wings the primal jest.
Her mothering darkness, broodingly,
Settles in downy softness round
Reluctant fledglings of her brood.
Tonight there are only stars:
Pin-pricks in a whirling, shrouded globe
In a dark dark room.
Such darkness demands great calm.
Much stumbling, stubbed toes, and smarting shins
Await the impatient rusher in or out.
Pray sudden paths of light
For all who panic in the night;
And for the pang that is a panther chained,
Weep parables of jungle into Central Park.

Ray Mizer

Pew Rack

I sit with the rest in the holy hush
Clutching at hymnal and hope
Awaiting the birth of love.
The choir restoreth my soul.
But hearing this burbling fathead here,
Pouring his rancid oil on the troubled waters below
Drowns me in doubt.
If once, by some glorious accident,
This unctuous apostate should slip,
And free the incandescent Word
Among combustibles such as we . . .
Our petulant pew would rock
And roll in flame like very hell.

Ray Mizer

Bell Weather

How many bells is it since all's well?
Heigh ho. There is a ringing in our ears.
The question goes by the (sounding) board.
At bedside, wharfside, curbside: bells.
Donne heard them plain, and after, Hemingway.
Poor Poe, you may remember, wrote of bells:
Their clanging rang in his head all night,
His pen a jingling clapper on the page.

How every brazen voice chimes in:
The bell man cries from land to land,
Casting his bell-shaped tones upon the waves,
Bouncing them back from charged ionosphere.
The bell buoy rocks in the foggy straits,
The signal bell clangs at the crossing.

When night encroaches on the day,
Then who will bear the bell away?
Bell-wether now turns Judas-goat,
Leading his flock to the killing floor.
Fear prowls unheard in the muffling dark,
And who will bell that creeping cat?
She springs from the slot at the automat,
She claws at our knees in the sullen street.

The Book unread, the candle dim,
Only the bell tolls ban—and straight,
The very deeps reverberate;
The shock waves pound at the aural gate,
Jar at the hinge of the weary will,
Till the high toll breaks us all.

The bell curve clamps down in a stern embrace
(and mind you're not caught on the ragged edge;
It's three deviations off the norm).

Bell weather indeed, sounding dungeon deep
From welkin of every steepled town
Hell's (dulcet) bells.

Ray Mizer

Flight Plan

A dead fly lay on the window ledge;
My breath dislodged it, and it fell
Into the arms of an upsoaring wind
And rose above the chimneys and disappeared.
Once in a way I even saw a roof
Deserting house and home
Go flopping off like some ungainly goose too long earthbound.
Often some startled rabbit, unaware,
In launching grasp of hunting hawk catapults skyward;
And even Ordovician rocks leap high
Impelled by outbound T.N.T.
The only question is when, you see.
So choose a trajectory, please,
And fasten your safety belts.
It's sixty G's at take-off.

Ray Mizer

The Far-traveller

Journeys, journeys without end
That always start from where we are
And almost never bring us home again.
The outer pointing toward some luring star,
Launching a lonely curve of space and time;
The inner probing the abyss of self,
The deep downdiving trace that plumbs within.
  How many phrases have they wrung from us?
  How many metaphors that shine so bright,
  Yet tritely rust still smoking from the forge,
  And even in the curing bath, reek dust?
How shall we speak the road? What image now
Will figure forth the constant wanderer?
Now Widsith, now Ulysses—old or new—
Childe Harold, Huck, or Cain, or Sgt. X?
Quixote, or Batman? Red Cross Knight,
Or Ishmael? It doesn't matter.
Sky is in his lungs,
Seas in his veins,
And continents in his bones;
Search he must, whether he go or stay.
Until the suns go out
He will dream maps and try to follow them;
His itching feet will blister endlessly,
With always one more beetling cliff to climb,
One plunging deep forever unexplored.

Ray Mizer

D.A.R.ling

The Daughters *(sic)*
of the American Revolution
('76 was ago nine score and eleven,
and all appearances notwithstanding,
you just know they couldn't *really* be)
But Yank a doodle dandy!
The ladies still preserved preserve
(it says right here in my sources)
the memory of those bright souls
who thumbed their gorge at Uncle George
and clobbered all the *status quo.*
So let us ever thankful be
for service duly rendered.
Old Thomas Paine of common sense
to comprehend the crisis would
one supposes, be forgot
long since, had these dear ladies not
kept his rebellious name a torch.
And that staunch leader of the rabble
(A plague on your pickled red herrings!)
Dark Crispus. Where would be his fame now, think you,
had not the flame of his memory
been tended so selflessly by these?
Go to! I say they are not sweet mummies,
Nor barnacles on ship of state. Salute these *filia.*
(I deny categorically that they are necro.)
A good revolutionist these days is hard to find.

Ray Mizer

First Manassas: 21 July, 1861

This stubbled, windswept hill is resting now;
Its quaint field-pieces staring open-mouthed
Across three hundred yards at other guns.
More than a century since last they spoke,
Shouting defiance, spitting the fertile seeds
Of the grapes of wrath. This is Manassas.
You'll find it referred to in history books as Bull Run.
Up there on the brow of the hill a bronze man sits,
Lonely and stern, astride a great bronze horse.
He sat there much the same one fiercer day.
They called him Stonewall for the way he stood.
It was less lonely then. This is the way:

The visitors and Congressman had come out,
The VIP's and correspondents, too,
To watch the show. McDowell turned the flank;
The Army of the Potomac was surprised;
Johnson and Beauregard and Lee despaired.
And then, against all reason, Jackson stood;
And seeing him stand, the wavering line grew firm;
The blue ranks faltered, sagged, retired.
It is no cause for wonder or for shame:
The fight so hardly fought, so nearly won,
Had met a wall that would not let them pass:
A Jericho without a Joshua.

And so, along the tangled, tortuous course,
The blue stream, stained red with dust and blood,
Flowed backward toward Washington and rest.
Many a Congressman got to the grass roots that gray day
By way of a uniformed voter's passing shove.
Predictions and politicians were sorely upset.
Had Johnson known in time the forest fire
Of panic his tired troops had set ablaze,
Manassas No. 2 might never have come.

But you have read the record, and you know
That Appomatox was a shattered world away.

Old Stonewall stands there still. No Army
Of the Shenandoah can recall him now.
And I, whose Grandfather Anderson marched in blue,
Marched—as some wry joke decreed it—straight into
    Andersonville,
And by some awful feat of will survived to march again—
I stand here looking at that inflexible face,
Remembering that indomitable will.
Jackson and Grandpa. They never met, surely;
(Rank made it unlikely as well as belief)
I put them together, the farm boy and general;
Real men, believing, and putting their all on the line.
Let them exchange grave salutes now, accepting mine;
Forgetting old scores and old scars.
For us now the weight of the aftermath,
For us now the unfinished task.

Ray Mizer

ARNOLD LAZARUS
JOSEPH COLIN MURPHEY
MICHAEL J. PHILLIPS
MALCOLM M. SEDAM
DAISY STIEBER SQUADRA

A House Named Sylvia

Wallflower by a mossy wall
in the shadow of maple and oak
she had stood too long neglected by swain.
We were going to do her over
—or so we thought.
We lifted her face and furnace
scrubbed out her coal-smoked soul
painted sun to her clapboards
and after a fashion becoming to ladies
dusted her shingles blue-white.

But she spat diamonds to the winds
stuck to her zinc hatpin
winked at clouds
made pacts with tornadoes.

To inform our maudlin sunshine
her brown stain bled
and soot drifted from her pores.

Darkly from her chimney she sent signals;
her messages came from the hearth.
Conversant in more than one tongue
though resisting polyglot
she rehearsed us in substitution drills.

At night she ran labs and seminars
leading us mim-mem into restoring
her original weather-warped front tooth.
We learned from her the language of welcoming.

With a clock in each mouth
she smiled at forests.
For Sylvia we went into woods
we never came out of.

Arnold Lazarus

Boneless on the Monon

Moving on the Monon in December,
throw away your bones.
Let snowy fields glide by,
the breakable glass ponds,
the skaters in molasses plaids
and honey pompoms,
courtesy of Currier & Ives.
Depend upon your team of diesels
to neigh along the rails,
their tow chains clanking,
their sledges swaying.
(On, Percheron! On, Charger!)
They may hoot at V-8 horses
stalled at crossings,
buried in snow sidings,
but you will move . . .
move past silos, corn cribs,
hogs magnificent in mufti,
and on thin stilts the formal water
blessing out the towns
of Battleground and Chalmers
Rensselaer and Hammond.
Near the Windy City
(past sticks and stones)
if snow whips up bad names
it will not harm your bones:
Anaesthetic with tobacco
all equestrians pull boneless
into Dearborn and Van Buren.

Arnold Lazarus

Traveler's Agent

Cradling a swan white telephone
in the curve of her Leda-lovely neck
but bussing the moment's silence mauve
with her country-store placebos and asides
("where there's life there's hope")
she confirms at last my space
in the sullen clabbered sky.
While her sweetcream smile, flush, ripeness
bursting decolleté et ceteris paribus
lure clichés to a thousand deaths,
her "life-hope" oracle sounds right,
suddenly, above the crashes
blackening this morning's paper.
So I must ask:
What hope may an inter-olympian loper,
booked out of this cornfield office,
out of these ice-cream snow mounds,
dispatched to the dairy sky, curd to whey,
entertain if he returns
(according to the myth) alive?

Arnold Lazarus

Great Lakes Gothic

This was our snowbound saltbox with smokestack,
the snow softening its sober outer posture
and giving the lie to drunken slants below.
Ceilings, walls, and lintels pitched tipsy on heavy seas,
the tilted floors sent us reeling into jigs,
and we bobbed sans benefit of cider,
or stuck together—taffies, tars, and avatars.
The galley had been added aft; above the anchor
of our yard this cabin rose on wooden pins,
naked as a barge in dry dock.
While our crew broke icicles from snowmen on the shore,
First Mate and I banked up around the ribs
to keep the winds from freezing decks and pipes.
But there were warmer moments forward
when, gathered at the window of our bridge,
we watched cake-frosted carriers and men-of war
float by on chainless bottoms and perilous drifts.

Arnold Lazarus

Decorations on a Japanese Fan

Side 1

Wearing autumn reds
and golds of maple driftings
ladies live in leaves

Side 2

Limbs turn lovelier
when leaves attach themselves to
  trees and dress the woods

Arnold Lazarus

"Travailler est mouir"—Prudhomme

One Ticket, One Dance (a penny opera)

"Wait," he cried, waltzing his muse around the outer fires,
the suburban embers, "are you a singer of songs yourself?
Do you compose or just audition?"

She caught her breath
on a flying trumpet, "Why what have I to do with all that jazz?"

"I don't know what or why or where; your looks excite
the sullen air; your body takes such reckless poses— "

"Don't take such liberties in public; a poet should be felt
not feeling; a poet should be heard, not seen;
a poet should not even mean.
Your ticket says we dance; so just keep dancing, Buster."

"I thought at first that I had breached you;
alas, I haven't even reached you."

"One moment, please, before you leave,
who *are* you? Who, in Hell, do you think you are?"

"I wish I knew," he smiled,
dying again in her embarrassed arms.

Arnold Lazarus

That Morning and Evening Sun

I

The day begins with the sun
through trees. I breakfast
and shave in the dazzling rise of life
coming up on an interval
of hurry which never is early enough.

We arrive at the citadel where the birds
still nest in the fall trees.
We climb to the level of learning.
The air is chill and freezes
the warm wish in our eyes.

We meet the gazes of the young.
Their unmade beds
smile still within their minds.
Sleepily they move in the sun.
Their flesh is slow and beautiful.

Their youth is covered with color
and in patches of hastening motion
they make abstractions on the Mall;
their shadows fall classward
and frighten mockingbirds.

The tower of this hill of light
rises in the sun through razzles
of cloud drifting away westward.
The sun is on the clock's face
and wakens eternal questions.

II

The day ends with the sun
slanting late, a cool death
of life to an interval.
And I have followed since dawn
this long thread of time.

I remember a child
and mother in Virginia stone,
pink and still, called "Continuity."
I remember a Feininger shaft
of light and sailboats.

I remember a black marble
venus, whose hips
were soft as life, and dreams
fell from a bronze caryatid
whose weight was the world.

I remember a child's eyes,
a woman on a bicycle
whose skirts made a flight
of flesh in sun. I remember
a girl crying over spilt grades.

There is a softness in sunset,
the colors run like tears. There is
a going-home tiredness in my mind.
My brief case is heavy still
with this day's answers to everything.

Joseph Colin Murphey

A Noise of Battle

He shall cry, yea, roar.
He shall prevail against his enemies.

It is neither man nor beast
nor blackest devil

who wears the lesser gods upon his belt,
cold death-heads clanging as he cleaves the air,

as jewels, they, to his black zone of thunder.
These that have been stone

or silent image, citadelled, "immortal,"
grave aegis guarding all from storm,

they but encrust his vesture in the heavens.
Inscriptions mount the capitals of his temple,

designs of pagan festival in stone.
And in his mass their songs abound,

have come to sing all praises to this one.
Of Dionysus' flesh and blood ambrosial

dead remembrance has new name and form.
So all encompassing, he gorges all.

Joseph Colin Murphey

Pieta by Mantegna (1431-1506)

The body falls prostrate, heavy here,
And there is no angle able
To rise at this fulcrum:
Beyond terrestrial mechanics
It would lie forever,
A giant carcass whose strength
In death is like Gulliver
Lying in Lilliput.

Immobility becomes here a power;
As silence is never nothingness.
The pale perspective to the head
Brings sorrow abreast of life,
Looms large in the inert feet,
The foreshortened body.
This is a low-lying torso
Heavy with death.

As in the age of Mantegna: death
To his level, an equality
From which no one rises except God,
From whose heaviness all things descend
And who beyond Adam
Made covenant here with death,
A three-day pact this side Limbo
When all weight fell in this frame.

Joseph Colin Murphey

Ode to the Statue Who Found a Trade

A lone G.I.
Stands hard by the funeral home.
They use him in their ads.
He lends prestige to the house of death.

One foot on a stone, this rifleman
lounges quietly. No elan of battle
shines from his bronze eye.
Modest and withdrawn, he does not presume.

Across the street before the statehouse
the heroes of other wars rouse the air
with their silent battle cries, on horses
or high pedestals of courage.

Their prominence demands its glory.
Bronze sabres, swords gory with the patina
of long reverence, their gestures speak:
"How sweet to die for the causes of yesterday."

But the lone G.I. knows
that death is impersonal and unheralded;
the tiredness which comes before
that kiss is an undeserv'd torture.

His bullet was as anonymous as he.
And we preserve him thus in state
of tired resignation. How carefully
his demeanor hides a unique valor:

Where he rests and waits
Achilles in that screaming, baited air
would go mad with fear.
The thunder he hears now is eternal.

No seven days wonder then
that his grim body adorns no square—
no flare of trumpets but car horns
passing near and the scream of ambulances.

The burial firm has taken
a long term lease. There is a peaceful gain
for those who deal in death
and the G.I. did know this business.

Joseph Colin Murphey

Portrait of a Lady

This lady once worked
in her garden, hat, gloves
and sun-reddened face
beaming mid chrysanthemums.

She was not beautiful,
her garden was. It lay
by the sea, sophistication
in every bed and bloom.

There was no clod of earth
not turned each week. How she sweated!
She lost herself in field-hand labor
but kept a maid for housework.

When the heart attack came,
the sea with its furrows
and beds of whitecaps were all
she could see from her pillow,

till she finally escaped
that harrowed bed to sit in a chair
to look down on her garden
as in a mirror:

her red rose mouth needed color;
her hyacinth eye needed shadow;
her shrubbery had long wisps
of hair-blown spray.

I heard last week
that she sneaked by the maid
and found her hoe and rake.
The yard wears now its accustomed smile.

The wake is Tuesday and the guests
will say, "What a beautiful garden!"
She was a simple woman, a good neighbor.
Her husband is a millionaire and may remarry.

Joseph Colin Murphey

In Proper Mode and Reverence

Madonna and child:
in the age of such a fashion
I should paint you
rapt in the light
of Heaven's showering
hosts,

angels descending.
But now I say as you sit
here with my child
that being a poet's
love with his borne
incarnate song,

I would not
shame the perfect
recreating of what
exists in two,
now one, with
antique mode

or leave undone
the proper beautification
of what our love
has made of mortal
and of yet
immortal frame.

Joseph Colin Murphey

Golden Age

For Joey

And now comes
a baby centaur, three
years old, his body

a delightful
trembling of hoofs, a maned
thrust in the wind.

The exotic dance
of his feet and the blond
sheen of his hair in sun

make Homer come reborn
to sit with satyr eyes
smiling, never seeing

the cowboys and Indians
nor anything as mortal
as a child upon a stick.

He sees a god riding:
a glittering poet-dream
of horse and man.

Joseph Colin Murphey

The Beginnings of Flight

Me and my Merrilee

used to swing through childhood
trees of spring under the blue
sky on wings of laughter,

climbing hills and sliding
down long sand flumes of joy
wrapped in each other's arms to roll
in the surf, boy and girl unknowing.

Me and my Merrilee

growing, found days and days
of flowing music beneath the sea
in rubber suits of flippered feeling,
reeling in golding depths of coral.

Now for fear of ever calling
each other by anything less
than lover or being lost in the depths
of a loneliness as deep as sky or sea,

me and my Merrilee

dive through skies of whining
blue, asking why the hurtling
moments of our blinding dance
in air cannot last forever and be

like an endless kiss beneath the sea,
without the necessity for air, flippers
or even the awareness of

me and my Merrilee.

Joseph Colin Murphey

From a series of sky-diving poems:
The Man with a Parachute.

The Mirrors

(In the following five pieces I attempt to describe five paintings, and then the reaction of five people to them.)

The foxy mayor suggested this Brueghel
For my gallery. A helicopter view of a city square
Where the minute citizens are nailed by state
On paper with other data—"The Census."
And one sees them all over the place like dots
On a Seurat. To the city leader they seemed
Akin to the countless insects that swarmed
Around him in the city building all day;
He too enjoyed the advantage of a height,
And drew the whole city into his vision.

*

When my mistress saw the face of Van Gogh's
"Self Portrait" after our first love rites,
The red beard and the hair, the old blue coat,
And the frame in front of the terrible face
Made her think of me. "This is the fire that I expect,
And I will grow it in him with my fair body;
His forms will flame to fame and last like mountains."

*

A monastic friend, a man with mystical strength,
Saw the abstract Klee over my study table.
Three oddly shaped sea monsters give battle
In the midst of ocean, sky, and waves
To a warrior standing in a boat
With a lance in his comical hands.
The monsters battle the man, and the man the monsters.
But Klee is not very serious and neither was the monk.
My vegetarian friend was forced to smile,
This man who lives in poverty for the sake
Of studying eastern thought and merging with essentials,
And thinks the bitch battle of life is perhaps
An object for laughter. For once I agreed.

*

Ocean and nature are in back; the man, woman, and child
Stand in the foreground, the surf near their feet;
Figures are predominant in a blue picture called
"The Tragedy."
Picasso leaned the adult heads in a kind of despair
That brought up in my mother thoughts of her recent marriage.
"The pain of their faces—the pain of struggle together—
Accents the bond of the law that says two live together."

*

The Buffet sums up, this silly "Clown,"
The way that life tears men up.
We know the silly color, the tinted lips,
The charcoaled eyes, the green hair,
And the painted face only too well.
The colors are funny, grotesque.
So life hurts, our vision is clouded,
And we get almost nowhere with men.
This clown makes me cry.

Michael J. Phillips

Eight Meetings
A Poem of Universal Diction

I

And like a queen
who asks a boy into her palace
you took me
to your orchids, pearls, and roses
by the city
to your black hair and fragrant shoulders
under moon and sun
by the waterfall.

II

Beneath the sky
by the blue and green sea
the wind sang
and the tide rolled into us
under the high trees
where it is said
thunder and lightning were born
on an ancient night.

III

On the same day
my ear heard your voice sigh twice
in the sea shell
I broke between your fingers
and you pulled me down to you
to the tear on your cheek
and you said no
then we said
yes, yes, yes
as the rainbow came to your eyes.

IV

After a journey over red and orange deserts
and black nights in the open
I came to you one day
in the garden of lilacs
by the deep, clear pool
where you shed your clothes
and I looked on you
by the flamingoes and swans
over the lilies-of-the-valley.

V

Among the bright dancers
I saw you
in the night

and your slight garments of gold
shone in motion
the grace of the deer
curve of leaf
softness of hummingbirds.

VI

And I sang in my soul to you
I played music
for kings and queens
on the oriental carpet
in your secret chamber
where windows opened to evening
and the light of the stars
was on your breasts
and the rings of many loves
on a chain around your neck.

VII

Raving
I came from the winter tempest
to your warm hearth and bed
and there was food
grapes for my lips
ambrosial drinks
and your clothing was white.

VIII

Into the harbor
from lands beyond today
the fleet ships are coming
and people are chanting in unison
for our love
the feast is prepared for our families
your maidens and sisters are dressing
and the earth is rejoicing.

Michael J. Phillips

The Love Address

I felt new language soar
as your bright red shoes beat
a path among the dwarf
trees by the clear water;
You trembled like spring seed.

Smooth skins like yours can twist
man to good, and lurch
great poets to lasting
pitch. As of now my stake
is man's romantic search.

Beauty is not a wine
or women with white wings,
but your face over thin
blue cotton by this lake.
As you look, so I gain!

Michael J. Phillips

The Great Bordello

A wind blew a tree against the big red house,
Fish swam toward land, menageries spawned,
An old madame asked what he would spend,
And down the stairs marched five shapely girls,
One by one. A poet, a farmer, a builder,
A physician, and a scientist appeared.

Eleven fragrant people on the shaking earth
Watched a handsome lad take off his clothes,
Drop all his money on the stair, and say
"Watch for me world—I am man."
A lion in a zoo teethed on thick iron bars,
A hungry shark swam up to a young dolphin.

Michael J. Phillips

Desafinado

(For Allen Ginsberg, et al.)

Through this state and on to Kansas
More black than May's tornadoes
Showering a debris of art—
I saw you coming long before you came
In paths of twisted fear and hate
And dread, uprooted, despising all judgment
                        which is not to say
That the bourgeois should not be judged
But by whom and by what,
Junkies, queers and rot
Who sit on their haunches and howl
That the race should be free for pot
And horny honesty?
                        which I would buy
If a crisis were ever solved
In grossness and minor resolve
But for whom and for what?
I protest your protest
Its hairy irrelevancy
I, who am more anxious than you
            more plaintive than you
            more confused than you
            having more at stake
An investment in humanity.

Malcolm M. Sedam

The Quick and the Dead

As friends of the deceased
We stood outside the plot
And spoke of many things;
I said that I was a teacher
And it came out he was too,
Somewhere up North, he said,
Good community—good school,
No foreigners, Negroes, or Jews
In fact, he said,
No prejudice of any kind.

Malcolm M. Sedam

Regeneration

Something in me and the abiding dust
Loosed an imprisoned force
And I became a man at the age of twelve
Proclaiming myself above women
I decided to be a trapper up North
But tried the near creek first
Caught a muskrat that turned me weak
Cried boy tears then came back strong
Finding maturity was thirteen
Growing soft on animals and girls.

Malcolm M. Sedam

Lee Anne

(On Her Seventh Birthday)

Walking
This side of her
When trees are bare
And distance sharpens the cold
Into a clear necessity
A turning goodbye
As time reveals her role—
What calmness
Lies behind the voice
When she asks,
"Why are we walking this road?"

Malcolm M. Sedam

Al Bargaher

When that burst of flak
Tore off your wing
And sent you spinning through the sky,
You looked just like a maple seed
Floating into the water
On a bright May-day;

I'm sorry you were chosen
To remind me of Spring.

Malcolm M. Sedam

Abraham at Moriah

Trusting His promise:
Unto thy seed will I give this land;
I went on and on believing
That my descendants would be many
Like the sands among the sea,
That He would make of me a great nation;
I sired a son when I was very old,
Proved I had miracle powers
Perhaps so great I challenged even His,
For jealously He asked me for this son;
My will divined the purpose of the Rod,
No man would kill his son for any God,
And knowing well His promise I had blessed
I thought it time to put Him to a test—
And so with Isaac I traveled to that place
And took along a ram
Just in case . . .

Malcolm M. Sedam

Incongruity

Theirs is a house, a show place
Of antiseptic rooms marked:
His and Hers
With climb marks on his walls
And halls that lead to nowhere
(They wouldn't dare)
And yet they have three daughters
Which their friends assure me
Came naturally.

Malcolm M. Sedam

Joseph

Some things were never explained
Even to me, and of course
They would tell it His way
But I believed in her
Because I chose to believe,
And you may be sure of this:
A man's biological role is small
But a god's can be no more
That it was I who was always there
To feed him, to clothe him
To teach him and nurture his growth—
Discount those foolish rumors
That bred on holy seed
For truly I say unto you:
I am the father of Christ.

Malcolm M. Sedam

Progression by Thirds

The caterpillar winds
up great grass-stems steep.
Blind, the believing mind
must creep.

The chrysalis upcurls
calmly in dark.
Faith's eye expects the whirl-
wind spark.

But the butterfly's concern
is clearly wings.
New understanding burns
old things.

Daisy Stieber Squadra

Haiku for the Heaven-sent

The pink petals fall
upon the polished table
like friends' words on night.

Daisy Stieber Squadra

Lines for a Longtime Friend

(a villanelle)

Recite now in an antique tongue
your memories of childhood places;
recite our world when it was young.

Relive the tiger-wonder sprung
on us by birthdays, by strange faces;
recite now in an antique tongue.

Tell the berried summer hung
ripely in reach: bare feet, boat races;
recite our world when it was young,

unscarred by war, when ballads sung
about our hearths embraced all races.
Recite now in an antique tongue.

For Babel's tower, too soon begun,
rattles on tiers of tinwood braces.
Recite our world when it was young,

when we were lambs in a noon sun
of love too bright for shadow-traces.
Recite now in an antique tongue;
recite our world when it was young.

Daisy Stieber Squadra

Impression

A rainy day like this runs silver,
submerges in its silver self
horizon and hill and remembered sun,
sounds only seawords: fathom, reef,
shapes only mermaid syllables.

A sunny day unlike this slumbers
somewhere, sunsunk undersea
in Debussian shafts of cathedraled
light,
waiting a belled day's dong to rise
gleaming and gold, seasilver shaken.

Daisy Stieber Squadra

A Poet on Her First Acceptance

Wind me a wreath from laurel boughs;
loose the bands that bind my hair;
call in harpists to harp now;
let lyrics blossom everywhere.

Yesterday I wore no ring,
found no silken gown.
Today the palace courier brings
an invitation from The Crown

to work syllabic filigree
along a balustrade,
carve adjectives of ivory,
definitives of jade.

Wind me a wreath from laurel boughs;
loose the bands that bind my hair;
call in harpists to harp now;
let lyrics blossom everywhere.

Daisy Stieber Squadra

December Landscape

Time of thin sun, time of the earth's turning
toward winter and quiescence and still sleep,
time of birds in flight, of sudden burning
brush-fires on bare beaches where some few keep

sharp rendezvous with solitude. The tide
sucks scattered shells back seaward and the sea
shakes from its lion's mane those gulls that ride
its foaming crest too far or brazenly.

No child grins from the beach-pines; no white sail
bobs on the blue horizon. Only cold
looms, as dry leaves crumble and daylight fails.
It is time now to build new warmths for old.

Daisy Stieber Squadra

Bach Discovered

Pillar by vertical pillar chords
hold horizontal melodies;
note by tremulous note, now words
fit dome and spire. Antiphonies
form flying buttresses for thought
to mount upon, to reach out where
the stroking birds of sound are caught
up in cathedral stillness. There,
I unearth keys to inner doors,
unlocking concepts vast as sky;
larks sing never heard before
and bright tonal lilies lie
by the thousands on the land,
waiting eager, empty hands.

Daisy Stieber Squadra

Fragments from Bethlehem

Stardust, dust of one
meteor falling
down on America's midwest,
mix with this soil;
merge with soya and corn;
make of our farmers
sowers of sublime seed,
growers of beanstalks
bursting with unique fruit
whose meat once tasted
turns each taster: prince
of mankind's peace.

Stardust, pieces of far
planets falling
down on our war-torn world,
your fall begun
billions of light years gone
to blaze one moment
in Sesquicentennial skies
—why did you come?

Daisy Stieber Squadra

Throughway Nocturne

Dark is a jungle. And what Cortez
dared cut this concrete swath through wilds
of buildings thick as Birnam Wood,
bricks tall enough to block the sun?
Whom credit so? No impasse-threat
thwarted this throughway's spinning, bridged
as is each pit with perfect arc
in parabolic steel enforced
by that same art of buttressing
which pinnacled cathedrals through
the crumbling of dry centuries.

And now my car, a great cat, comes
from copse to clearing, far to fringe,
sleek and gold-eyed and crouched to spring
deftly into the mainstream, fury
of forward engine-thrust: a purr
speaking the panther's joy in running.

Daisy Stieber Squadra

WILLIS BARNSTONE
THOMAS N. MEEK

Kaminia-Hydra

Mill, chapel, oven on the hill,
white walls and tile, blue windowsills
the color of the sea below.

Under the godless sun the town
is a glare of cubes. The air blows
with smells of salt, dung, jasmin, heat.

Out of the rock heart of this island
seven round fig trees face the sky
and an acacia cools the well.

The tiers of homes nap in the noon
like a deserted amphitheater
around the bay—O town of light!

A peasant born here will soon leave
the light to die, yet when the walls
get dark they are washed white again.

Light and tedium. A pomegranate
slowly bursts in the heat, its bloody
seeds are eyes peering at the wind.

Willis Barnstone

By the Bullhorn Mountain: Mykenai

The dayfall moon
glares over the treeless mountain, the cliff,
and dark bands of fields and fir groves,
and a young olive tree by the rock wall.

Some cicadas clamor.
They scream in the stubble and rub the stars
vibrating within the intense
reaches of their own solitude. The sphere

is seen but unchanged
by men. Owls hoo. Wind carries time from branch
to branch of the cemetery
cypresses and down to the invisible

scheme of anthills,
moles and fig-roots and the anonymous worm.
A town blinks far, still; while the night
of noisy nature clamors in its fire.

Willis Barnstone

Standstill

I have nothing to say. I hear a few
birds through the rubber trees. I remember
the new moon hanging over the daytime sea,

and a few days ago, there I was lost
in the mountain rain-forest with mangoes
lying yellow and spotted with disease

on the leaves and muddy earth. Emptiness.
Though closed in by sensual beauties of
a ripe landscape, a sky fragrant with wind

and salt, and sea whose gray-purple contours
bend across the earth with grace and mystery,
I am still a shell—with little passion,

and moved mainly by desire for desire.
In this room, with my sly mosquito friends,
I hear birds chirping through the rubber tree.

Willis Barnstone

Explosion

Trees are blue,
as old winter
starts. The cold sky
coughs over junkyards
and blasts the night of frogs.
Cold evening.
Among the black bushes
we are numb and unable to think.

We have a messy dream about sun
hanging in the dark,
and are confused in our cold bodies
small in the snowy
underbrush. We can't
think our way above
the sky pounding down.

In the blue trees
we dream of a spasm of light.
Mud goes through our soggy shoes
and we convulse alone.

Willis Barnstone

Going Outside

Enough now. My head black with words,
I know I do not know and close
the door behind. Sun in the streets
and pigeons on the bright cement.
The morning splashes on the ground,
against the ancient orange wall.
Blast of donkeys, cocks. Children scream.
The air glares back with burning dust.
For a slow moment now I watch
red flowerpots on the sunny ledge.

Willis Barnstone

Reflection on Suicide

Nothing is worse. Pity the suicide,
for we are animals who love the sun,

yet we who wait out death, in godless time,
live with terror (always hoping to know).

In hating life he closed his eyes: in one
mechanical gesture, forgot the dark.

Pity him for his loss, for his deadly wound,
yet his dying was peace, perhaps, with less dread

than ours who hunger for each hour of light.
Pity him who ran to death, and us who run.

Willis Barnstone

Lapland

The roots of the earth protrude
down into the pinegray ocean
and up into the glacial snow.

There are not many fir trees
as we push into the unreal
north. We are beyond the green

and on nude scrubby earth again.
Here where snow yawns into the
sea, and air is clean like fish,

distance and form and seasons
are more true than the odd boat
or village. Time. This land is

dream—planet where almost no one
is—or if real, then quick cities
south are dream before the slow

iceland. At night sunshine floats
on big mountain ribs of snow;
gulls cry and cod run in the ocean.

Willis Barnstone

I.

"We are now passing through
the fog belt."
(they grow fog here
in the hollows
and river valleys
at night.
And they gather it
in the mornings;
to sell at circuses
as cotton candy.)

Thomas N. Meek

II.

My own little
world
My fuzzy little
four-by world
When I take my
glasses
off . . .
Little
my own
WORLD

Ah!!

Thomas N. Meek

III.

The clouds have died.
Collapsed, they fell
to earth
Gushing out their
Last Gassy Breaths.
Once they floated,
great mats of
sky-weed
Great gassy
amoebic forms
Sucking up
aerial plankton
as they smiled.
Now they lie
deflated, still,
in the low pockets of
the earth.
(We wade through their corpses
as we walk.)

Thomas N. Meek

IV.

It's Winter now
And all the Autumn leaves
have died and gone
to Heaven or to Hell;
the elm-trees wave
their branches
naked now,
And the robins of
Springtime-Summer
have left us
lonely cold.
But all the faithful sparrows
(wretched little paupers)
have stayed to sing
a greeting to the sun.

Thomas N. Meek

V.

She
breathed into my
still mind
padding like a kitten
softly; siamese.
How honest the smiling of her eyes on me!
A lock of hair, wind-blown,
caressing the corner of
her smile . . .

The same wind fanning the spark
of my longing
to touch her,
to kiss her,
to possess her.
Yes.
For I am a man.
But, more important,
more urgent,
more joyful
to be here,
now,
with her
looking at her
speaking softly
sitting quietly doing nothing
worshipping NOW
with her
With my mind
touching her mind
with my soul
and her soul
entwined in a lovers' knot.
I smile softly
to myself,
but am no longer surprised to see
my smile reflected
on her lips.
Or was it her smile
reflected on mine?
All wonderment is
buried in my
Laugh of Gladness.

Thomas N. Meek

VI.

When the Full Moon
wears a halo,
When the cones of
Lamp-light
stand in rows along the streets,
When snow fills my nostrils
and filters down my collar;
when all is silent and
Serene,
The sacred cats go walking.
(Step lightly, love,
And lift your feet high
as you go through the powder.
And crouch low
when the wind ruffles your fur.
But walk on; your beauty is untouchable,
your fluidity
the Joy of the Night.)

Thomas N. Meek

ELIZABETH A. BEHNKE
MILDRED LEISURE IRVIN
JEANNE EAGLES McCORMACK
FRANCES BROWN PRICE

road under construction travel at your own risk

I

I have a thing for you:
it is called a mind
and it is a ticket to the dark tower
it is a tiny thread suitable for 1) maze
2) amazement
it is a white line from pillar to post
and a fragile fluff seeding a newborn northern land.

II

Highly irrelevant
and afflicted with all the detachment
of an empty coffin
my thoughts lie in wait
for ribbons of yesterday's
perceptions
hells
and, of all the ugly questions,
loves.

Elizabeth A. Behnke

Finding

I

I thought my heart a castle
and built around a wall;
I hid myself within it,
unseen, unsought by all.
I set my flags a-flying
to show I needed none;
the colors flew with wind and rain,
but faded in the sun.

Stone is hard and faithful;
the wall was hard and strong.
It would be standing yet, but for
a heart—a hand—a song.

II

Sleep well, my love, and rest ye
until we meet again;
and I will think upon ye,
my bonnie prince of men,

and hold your heart a-keeping,
and hope you think of me;
for I'll be home a-waiting
when you come o'er the lea.

Elizabeth A. Behnke

ages ago in the twisted wood

ages ago in the twisted wood
a small face creeping toward the mountain
saw a song and sang it;
ages ago in a bloody forest
a hand reaching for water
carved a curve of sunlight
ages ago a stone stood by the river
and the stone is by the river today.

Elizabeth A. Behnke

The Sun's Setting Gold

The sun's setting gold is river on the run
and the sound of dusk is the
          song of riotous pebbles
while somewhere beyond heron's call
the night is a chant of a
          gray wind
over a runestruck sea.

Elizabeth A. Behnke

Monuments

The Mind believes in pomp and power
And gold and silken things;
It longs for walls and laurel wreaths
And power and peacock wings.

The heart is such a gentle thing—
So tied to by-gone days,
It sees a rose and weeps again
For old familiar ways.

Each treads the path and finds the grave
In darkness, all alone;
The heart lives on in loving words—
The mind in senseless stone.

Mildred Leisure Irvin

October

I heard your song at the break of day
Above the wild geese calling,
And laughed with joy to be up and away,
Down to the creek where the willows sway,
On to fields where stars are falling.

The cares of the world are not for me!
The flaming woods is waiting
And, standing under a maple tree
Is just the one I long to see
While Dawn is hesitating.

We're off to the lands where fairies dance—
My hand is in your keeping;
Gay elves flit by without a glance
As we ride October's vast expanse
While the rest of the world is sleeping.

We'll paint the pumpkin's golden hue
And drink the wine-red weather!
Our every hope is grave and new
And life's complete for me and you
When we take to the hills together!

Mildred Leisure Irvin

Another poem by Mildred Leisure Irvin is included in the humorous poetry section.

The House a Poet Built

The ground floor is level
stolid plank
a Breughelian inscape:
flagons, books, and chairs
casually arranged.
Even this conscious clutter
is slow flux
is caught
in random flashes
of perfection
nailed into my forehead.

The second floor is flimsier.
Furniture comes alive
and floats about,
thus often takes me by surprise.
Drawers yawn, crooked curtains smile—
a disarray of poltergeist at work.
This play of dream
the unexpected
lures the curious child
to that turn on the stair
where he hesitates.

If we dare the private dark
a sudden ledge beyond the rise
wainscot and rafters almost meet
and relics of real moment
rattle in the walls;
but looking down
uncoiling steeps
reaching into cellar depths—
steps fall away
beneath our feet
accident exceeding fate.

Pull down the stairs
to reach the tower
with its high ceiling-floor
of glassy sky:
green meteors of sea fern
wash across the crystals
of my mind—
a room of clear unfathomed height.
My eyes swim up through liquid light
to grasp in brief delirium
an aquarium of stars.

Jeanne Eagles McCormack

The Orchard

Rustling
through listless leaves, wind
dancing soft-shoe on shingled
roofs gentle stirs the
orchard.

Swaying
the boughs, a waltzing
gale soon rides in a gallop
branches bobbing with
apples.

Rain lashed
to a hurricane
frenzy: kermess of apples
spattering the ground
turned wine.

Jeanne Eagles McCormack

Our Equipage: A Riddle

We are all
like Gaul
three parts divided,
a horse
a carriage
a driver.

The horse
untrained
jerks free
of the rein,
galloping off
none the wiser.

The carriage
collapsing
falls apart,
smashing
downhill
unguided.

The driver
explains
with three lies
and a snort.
Who is master
is never decided.

Jeanne Eagles McCormack

Springtide

Opaque and pale
the pollen
of emerald moons
sifting
to the ground
dusts the tops
of trees and shrubs
in chalky waves.

Wild cherry
plum, redbud
and pear
appear like clouds
in a mackled sky,
open out
irridescent
upon a dusty ocean.

Beyond the moon
archipelagoes
glow through the mist
candescent green:
pearl and coral islands
bloom across
great swelling
seas of spring.

Jeanne Eagles McCormack

The Slowly Shaping Heart

You are the slowly shaping
heart of man.

Once, only embryo, you crawled
from murk of swamps
up unmarked time to move
erect, esteemed; to tower
above Neanderthalic sires,
and probe with fissioned hope
for secrets stored in stars.

But jungle tentacles still cling—
the pain of change endures.

You are the woman beggar pleading
for balm of dignity
in Boston, Bombay, Hong Kong—
the dark-skin child bleeding,
his spirit bruised and cut
on color-sharpened doors.

You are the slowly shaping
heart of man.

Frances Brown Price

On Wings Barely Dry

We are the frightened, rebellious voices
chorusing recklessly where evil clings,
eagerly leaving cocoons of our youth
desperately fanning the damp from our wings.
We are idealists, homespun and foreign,
dreaming and daring, awhirl on time's wheels;
we are the flag-burning, rioting students
endlessly, earnestly storming bastilles.
Curb our excesses but understand why;
pity us, cheer for us, frightened, courageous,
lifting the future on wings barely dry,
our blood on the banners as we pass you by.

Frances Brown Price

In What New Bethlehem

How long must Herod-fear
destroy for power,
deny divinity
of peace to flower?

How soon will shepherd winds,
star led through night
along the racial rocks
of rift, find right?

In what new Bethlehem
will Christ, reborn,
begin to wear the crown
and not the thorn?

Frances Brown Price

Too Sad for Spring

I watch the snowflakes swirl their last ballet,
then scurry from the roof like small white mice;
I hear spring's bagpipes skirl not far away,
and see the silo tip his cap of ice
in courtly welcome. The pasture pond
breaks frozen bonds to smile. But all the while
my heart stays winter-cold with loss beyond
the wand of living spring to reconcile.

Frances Brown Price

Honorable Mention

TERRY CAULEY
LOUIS J. FOERDERER
ALICE ELIZABETH FRAIN
JOYCE GULLESON
EMMA BLOSSER HARTZLER
EARL HUGHES
JOHN PRATT
MARY ROE
MARY D. SARE
CORDELIA SPITZER
RUTH TORBERT
MARGARET TRUSLER

I Shall Love Lightly

I shall love lightly, as the petal of a rose
Falls soundlessly upon the dew-drenched grass.
I shall avoid crass complications and untidy entanglements.
I shall love for tonight and not for tomorrow.
I shall love the shadow and not the substance,
For shadows are far lovelier than substance,
And also they are much easier to leave behind.

Terry Cauley

Circumstances

Long, long ago, as a very small boy,
I slept in a trundle-bed in a large room
In which on winter nights a great fire had blazed
In the huge and cavernous fire-place.
At bed-time the fire was covered with ashes
To save its precious germ for the morning.
But after the lamp was out the coals still glowed through
the ashes;
And once in a while even a blaze erupted like a volcano.
Then the big room leaped into vast magic and fantastic
shadows
Of the rafters did ghost dances in the murk under the roof.
Each time this happened I liked it so much that I vowed
to myself,
"I'll stay awake till it happens one more time."
But ultimately, of course, this vow, like so many other
good ones,
Was broken because of circumstances beyond my control.

Terry Cauley

Smoke in the Evening

The gray-blue smoke on evening sky,
Wood-smoke from crackling, dancing fires
New kindled on the farmhouse hearths,
Against the rising chill of autumn's breath,
It drifts upon the crisping air,
Spreads thinly over windy woods,
And thus proclaims man's sure defense
Against the cold of winter night.

It bears no bond in common with
The sooty pall of tortured towns;
It does not blot the cleanly sun
Or settle down to clog the lungs
Of children frail and tautly thin,
Or plague the lives of women tired
From hanging dingy washing on
The lankly ugly fire-escapes.

The smoke of cities is a curse
Laid down on men for gorge and glut,
For grasping greed of mill and shop;
But thin wood-smoke on country air
Bespeaks a boon to human-kind,
A promise of security.

Terry Cauley

If You Be Moved to Grieve

If you be moved to grieve that I am gone,
Think not that I am truly dead;
For this good soil and this lush rain
That lave me toe to breast to head
Will surely serve as well for me
As for the seed, the plant, the tree.

The God who deals the roiling round
Of ceaseless and unmortal change
Will do not less for my poor bones,
Laid here in nature's runic range,
Though blind to smile and deaf to grief,
Than for a lately fallen leaf.

Terry Cauley

Troop Ship

As I rose from steerage and came on deck
The clean, washed air ripped away the taint
Of the vomit and kerosene reeking hold.

The hypnotist stars lured me into the night,
Clutched at my shoulders in spray-sweet embrace.
The flèche of the bow, a whetted knife,

Ripped through layers of silver embroidered cloth,
(Dark violet, royal and azure blue;
Shredded hems were bleached aqua and billowing white)

Which fluttered and laved the tempered prow.
The phosphorus trail was the tail of a kite
Which tugged at the thread of the endless night—

So close seemed the heavens, I stretched to my height . . .
"Are you sick?" said the sergeant.
"No. Lost," I replied.

Louis J. Foerderer

The Dingy on the Flow

Four jolly sailors on the flow, Ho! Ho!
Four jolly comrades in a boat.
And what t' them did happen when the wind set t' blow?
What t' them did happen when the storm let go?

Well . . . one rowed with a broken oar,
One panned with 'is hat in 'is hand,
One prayed to 'is God for land,
And the other laughed as 'e rode, Ho! Ho!
The other laughed as 'e rode.

This'n maybe 'e was crazy and maybe 'e was lazy:
For 'e coolly sat as the rage did blow.
('e sat there hummin' while the water laid 'em low,
And noted what 'e saw in the storm, let go.)

While the wind, set free,
Blew the dingy t' the quay.
And each of the four, once ashore,
Thanked 'imself for the savin' of the boat, Ho! Ho!
'IMSELF for the savin' of the boat.

Louis J. Foerderer

Indecision

After a storm of uncertain decision,
Worried wondering, wishing wild,
The mind seeps silently back from a shore,
Recedes, a damp, calm, resolute void,
Like the spirit of revelry dead from a night
Of frenzied desiring—a dirge, then a flight!

The white fevered surf is resolved in cool green.
Just under the sea's silver spangled caps
Fish silent slither, determined, devout,
Heeding unshackled the siren's sweet call.

The bark lurches longingly, grudgingly out.
Oars lightly dipped push whirlpools from the bow.

Louis J. Foerderer

Birds

Whirling, twirling, ringing 'round,
Singing, winging furrowed ground,
Upward, sky-wide, wing-whipped, free,
Sun-bound, world rimmed, mist-dimmed flight,
Earthbound, mate-sound, rose-tipped tree,
Molting, scolding, tempting, fright,
Envied, hunted, covied, flushed,
Spring sings, firstlings, weak-winged, crushed.

Louis J. Foerderer

The Tree of Knowledge . . .

Pull on the shroud of endless twilight and mourning,
Come live with me.
Sing dirges.
They can be love songs,
Epitaphs, poetry,
And flesh, the hangman's tree.

Evade the liens of conformity,
Yes!
Exult in expulsion,
FREEDOM . . .
Then,
Alone,
Your back to the rim of life,
Damn the upright tree!

Won't you come live with me?

Louis J. Foerderer

Death

A leaf is dying,
Then descends,
And pierces his brother—
Or skims lightly to its pyre—
Mocking gravity as it lingers in mid-air
In confusion—
But, drops eventually—
Its descent complete.

Upon stony earth its bed,
Even then disturbed in its last nourished moments
To be stepped upon.

Alice Elizabeth Frain

Bones of My Brothers

I'll take my course among the bones of my brothers
And watch the faded lamp betray the night.
Among the refuse of a life once spent,
Of dreams once dreamt,
Now to no avail these men, but me—
May I borrow their bones
And cling to their dreams.

Carefully, I pick my way
Choosing quality to mold one man,
To shape no soul, but to pattern one life.
Out of those before, I graft my mind.

Alice Elizabeth Frain

Among Men

Here they are,
All of them searching.
Each one peering over his neighbor's head
Into a dusty future.
Brushing one against the other,
But feeling no one.
Pushing in panic at times.
Far away some see a light,
A hallowed sun of content.
Then the surge.
But, alas, no one moving far.

It's so dark back here in the crowd,
And the people mob so.
Funny you can't see the people.
Maybe if you look
And feel,
And communicate,
And now we are.
And funny no one's searching anymore.

Alice Elizabeth Frain

Elysium

I saw him choose a crooked stick
and beat the ground—then I wondered and feared.

Later, as I picked tiny berries
among the brambles, I heard him sob.

I crept over and cocked my ear to hear
his jumbled muttering;

He sat there amidst dust and dirt,
his face nearly touching the ground.

He seemed to be asking pardon ever so tenderly,
yet so profusely did he speak.

His face was beautiful and innocent,
and no longer was his mouth funny
and twisted in that horrible grin.

His eyes were pools of blue water,
salty with tears, and not wickedly
piercing as before.

Strangely, I no longer feared, nor wondered
about him, for now I understood.

I felt at that moment that heaven
must be very near.

Slowly I bent down, and as our eyes met,
our minds became one, I believe.

He touched my hand, and my berries spilled.

Alice Elizabeth Frain

After Rain

A million leaves
Sigh restlessly
Shedding tears
Over the past rain.

Joyce Gulleson

Willow

The weeping willow fountains forth
In gentle soft green sprays
Whose mild and mellow rhythms
Count off the summer days.

Joyce Gulleson

Icicles

Shattered alabaster;
Gleaming crystal shafts.
Winter's royal diadem
Atones for icy blasts.

Joyce Gulleson

Strip-Trees

Right in the middle of our front yard—
She stands there
Coquettishly
Unpinning her copper-gold tresses,
Bare limbs so gracefully swaying
In lacy black-webbed underwear.
I watch
As brazenly she shrugs and undresses.

Emma Blosser Hartzler

These Make Freckled Faces

Dapples of dawn gold,
Flecks of radiant sky
Filtered
Through an autumn maple,
Sieved sunlight
Settled—
These make freckled faces.

Dust off antique gold,
Shadows of bronzed bowls
Spreckled
By soft candle glowing,
Copper coin dots
Scattered—
These make freckled faces.

Dew gems on marigolds,
Buzz of bumble bee
Reeling
In tawny tiger's claw,
Burnt orange poppies
Peeling—
These make freckled faces.

Dulcet touch of songlit gold,
Vibrant tones and silence
Tossing
'Tween honey throated thrushes,
Amber echoes
Bouncing—
These make freckled faces.

Spice drops of orchard gold,
Cinnamon and raisins
Sprinkled

Throughout a hearthwarm loaf,
Brown sugar lumps
Sifted—
These make freckled faces.

Cat's eyes of green sparked gold,
Toads and tadpoles
Splashing
In star kissed ponds at moonlight,
Cloaks of lady bugs
Splattered—
These make freckled faces.

Lantern flies of flashing gold,
Rust off olden buckets
Battered
By an awkward guernsey,
Storm stressed straw stacks
Shattered—
These make freckled faces.

Nuggets of panned gold,
Strands of broken coral
Tinkling
Into bubbles dancing,
Aurora borealis
Twinkling—
All these make freckled faces.

Emma Blosser Hartzler

Once I Was in New Orleans

Once I was in New Orleans
On New Year's night.
Large Christmas candles stood on Canal Street.
There were many beautiful women,
And for every beautiful woman there was a man,
With a few sailors left over
And a soldier.

. . .

I had a hamburger
And went down to the ferry . . . .
Ferry boats crossing the Mississippi,
Ferry boats tooting to each other from opposite shores,
Always meeting in midstream
And neither turning back.

. . .

I saw a man lying in front of a night club.
He was trying but getting nowhere.
His false teeth were lying on the sidewalk.
The policeman came and put his teeth in his pocket,
And took the gentleman for a ride in his wagon.
The girls were laughing behind a glass door.

. . .

I was in New Orleans
On New Year's night,
And my train was to leave in an hour.
There are four things I would like to know:
Is there still a man
For every beautiful woman,
With a few sailors left over?
Did the ferry boats get on the same side of the river?
Did the woman at the night club laugh
When she had to pay the bill?
Do the large candles stand on Canal Street
Each New Year?

Yes, there are six things I want to know.
What do they do in the French quarter?
And do the trains still run to New Orleans?

Earl Hughes

A Bargain in Berries

Tom Jones sells blackberries at two-fifty for five.
Five gallons that is.
"A bargain for you," he says.
"For you earn two-fifty in two hours
On your public job."
But I, too, have a blackberry patch,
And I can pick five gallons in a long half-day.
Glory hallelujah!
What do I know about arithmetic?
I feel good picking my own blackberries.
It's God feeding his little children.
I am one with the birds and the bees
And I love everyone better in a berry patch.
The most luscious berries never see the bucket,
And my mouth is the color of a blackberry.
Glory hallelujah!
Selling blackberries at two-fifty for five,
Tom Jones, too, should say,
Glory hallelujah!

Earl Hughes

Second-growth Timber

Brush land was cheap, and a depression then
Made clearing land scarce worth the time it took.
But he was young. He cleared and dreamed of when
Wide new ground fields would open like a book
With pictures of green grass and cattle stock,
Of gardens and a house, a country girl
Appearing there beside his chopping block
For hickory sticks to fry the highland squirrel . . .
Spring came. He heard a lonesome whistle blow
Confusing all his dreams. The wild geese said,
Somewhere tough butted white oaks do not grow.
Somewhere you'll earn big currency instead . . .

Today he sits beside a railroad track,
And wishes for a train to take him back.

Earl Hughes

Paging the Janitor

And the great shall be confounded
By the small.
Let the wedding continue.
The semi-darkness candlelight
Flows with that of the organ.
The black robed minister enters
With the groom,
And the ring bearer,
All in step with the solemnity of the ceremony.
The linen is laid and
"Here comes the bride, here comes the bride,"
Is struck from the organ.
And we fail to see the solemnity of the hour
At the glory of her entrance
Making glad the sight of the people.
But the sonorous voice of the preacher
Restores the dignity of sobriety,
And the wedding is solemnized
In the presence of God.
Far above the altar
A cobweb swings from the fixtures.
A cobweb swings gently,
A cobweb swings,
And swings,
In the breeze.

Earl Hughes

The Scoundrel

Chickens are important birds;
Men feed them
And rob their nests of eggs.
The hawk is a scoundrel.
God feeds the hawk.
When God turns his head the hawk feeds himself.

. . .

I heard two hawks cry down in the woodlot,
The squatters!
They must have baby hawks to feed.

John Fleming with a gun,
Cheered by hawk-hating ancestors,
Shot the two hawks from their nesting tree.
Maybe he saved the life of a dominecker chicken.

Chickens are important birds;
Men feed them
And carefully place a glass egg
In their nests.

I tell you hawks are scoundrels.
Look here.
I'll show you what's inside this hawk,
John Fleming said.

. . . . two snakes!

The dirty scoundrel!
Why should a hawk live on snakes?
Snakes eat mice—chicken-feed eaters.
Chickens pay for the feed they eat.
Chickens are important birds!

. . .

When God turns his head,
Man takes things into his own hands.

The baby hawks wait in a forgotten nest.
The winter winds whisper to the nest,
But there is no reply.

Earl Hughes

Campus in Late March

Stretching their tight-budded limbs, great trees
In cool expectant mist submerge their tendrils.
Selectively, efficiently, they breathe,
For only sense-slaved animals must writhe
In fecund scent that, all-pervading, fills
The breast of Being, and impregnates hills
With stirring seeds strange-spawned of restless ease.

Smell the pungent tang of Saxon dare—
A blend of river oil and brackish places
Damp drifting up the length of Delaware
To hold and mingle stench of men and seas
On brewing hills remote from both of these.
Young knights-of-promise under oak-gnarls there
Cast down their swords, and raise pubescent faces.

John Pratt

Fields of Champagne

Fields of Champagne, sown hill on hill with crosses—
Fields of crosses, stretching to the sky,
Crosses, crosses, stark and meaningless:
In blank insipidity a token—
On the good rich land a wasteful symbol—
A chance obeisance to the dead,
Hammered deep into the muck
Where lemmings lie.

Yes wave on wave they come at various periods—
In snaking ranks their silhouettes flow, twisting,
From the smog and slum of cities,
And matchbox houses vomit out these shadows
From suburbs, endless suburbs of the cultureless people.

Then they are placed in geometric rows
And bang • bang • the weird reminder grows
Across the hills where chaos grew and swelled
Are planted staring symbols by the man
With tape, with thoughts of wine and food and bed,
And dim traditions of
A formal garden in the French manner.

Blip-blip, a pause, then blaaap—
The heedless *voiture* crosses no-man's land.
Here asphalt settles into rows that jounce;
There, beaded bubbles on the surface bounce
(Aunt Frannie's on her holiday in Chicago).
While vine-leaves glisten with a pagan green
Aunt Frannie's in the Pump Room to be seen
Made giggly by the blood of Uncle Ned.

Requiem

O strike the lyre and sing of heroes dead;
Bring in the meat upon the flaming sword;

Lift high the cup and quaff the juices down
Made fragrant with the blood of Uncle Ned!

John Pratt

Sonnet

I love the Earth, and then she swallows me
In clay and rot and cold remorseless rain
As if our love, indulged in sun-warmed fields
Will use me up in sweet releasing pain
Until, bound to her limp, my power yields,
And she, for longing, takes me in again.

By chance I love the Earth, and chance that love:
I would not spurn this union offered free,
And when I am expended on my love
I'll lie enfolded in her memory
Or weary-out the dripping aftermath,
My act forgotten, and its scene ignored.

So, like the Mantis though her nature be,
I'll love the Earth before she swallows me.

John Pratt

Okefenokee

Where a swamp crawls up to the roadway
And the black water lies in wait;
Where the swamp fox prowls
And the swamp ghost howls,
Who is to say what is hate?
Who is to say what is love,
When the gator bawls for his mate?

Where the swamp crawls off through the cypress
And the water lies dim and queer;
Where the hurricane sweeps
And the cottonmouth sleeps,
Who is to say what is fear?
Who is to say what is loathsome,
If the cottonmouth holds it dear?

Where a river is born in the darkness
And the moon scatters tokens of gold;
Where the coral snake hides,
And the diamond-back glides,
Who is to say what is cold?
Who is to say what is courage,
Where quicksand strangles the bold?

Where a stream coils slow by the hammocks
And wild palms pray to the light;
Where the mud turtle crawls
And the swamp bear mauls,
Who is to say what is right?
Who is to say what is murder,
As a swamp cat screams in the night?

Mary Roe

Desert Spring

Ancient desert sands
    bed of some forgotten lake—
What was its color?—
Bear giant forms with strange uplifted arms.
These wait in stoic, sombre pain
For hard-won birth of brilliant petaled flowers.

Mary Roe

Indian Graveyard

North of the Ajo Road,
Direction of Way Over There,
A trail leads off through the grey mesquite,
A trail leads off through the sand and heat,
And ends in a valley where
The graves are made of sticks and stones.
If you lift a rock you can see the bones
Of the Indian dead;
(With blanket, saddle or Stetson hat.)
Or maybe you'll see an old pack rat
As he barters a pebble for something bright:
A silver buckle which catches the light;
A silver buckle he cannot wear—
For old pack rats don't care.

Mary Roe

Honor Guard

I walk the Honor Guard;
Slow measured footsteps past his gleaming tomb.
I walk in honor of a man none ever knew.
Yet, deep in troubled silence, I believe
  he sometimes walks beside me
  in the far, lone reaches of an autumn night.
(With serious eyes, his tall and lanky form
  stands forth athwart the rainfall on his grave.)

And once he asked, his young eyes dull with fear,
"Whose bones lie there beneath that marble shell?
"What freak of awesome heaven or awful hell
  keeps you and me walking eternally
  in this slow, endless funeral march?"

"*I* guard the Unknown Soldier!" He replied,
"That explains *you*, but why an *I* here?"

Yes, sometimes in the far, lone reaches of the night
  when wind has howled and autumn leaves have rained,
  he walks beside me; walks with puzzled eyes,
  and never knows his own lost body lies
  in that pale tomb to which we both are chained.

Mary Roe

Author's Ridge

I climbed there softly
    and the low, low sun
    sent dusky rays beneath the march of trees.
Their honored bones are there, huddled along the ridge:
Thoreau, Hawthorne, Emerson, and Louisa May Alcott
    wrapped in cloth and lace and timely rot.

I wonder if they walk
about the hill, when all who come to gawk
(like me) have gone away?

Why, yes, that slouchy, unwashed ghost . . . . .
I see him rather well.
He speaks: "Did you see what the hell
    they did to Walden's Pond?"
Emerson says primly, "I preferred good houses.
Thoreau was the beatnik of his day."

Hawthorne seems disturbed. "I wish they weren't here.
I wish they hadn't buried them so near."
Louisa, woman-like, sounds a different note:
"*You* never read a single thing I wrote."

Mary Roe

Advice to a Girl Graduate

Look straight, my darling.
Let your mind look straight
At things, and news, and other people's schemes;
At galaxies and stars, and painted dreams.

A heart may hurt,
May rail at God or fate;
But when a heart sees *whole,*
It cannot hate.

Mary Roe

Lay Poet's Lament

Wouldst we had never heard of style,
My pen and I.
We like to ply our wares in open cart
And trundle by;
Stopping now for sweet, unbridled word
That may resemble something old we've heard,
But there it is—for weeping or for joys,
Uncrusted by the brittle new alloys
Of sophistry, that are so strangely wrought
Paradigms so pure, we lose the thought.

Mary D. Sare

Two Cloaks to Wear

My love is two cloaks: one is gossamer and green
With a soft embedded interlacing sheen
Of gold, that so exotically and sharply silhouettes
The time when once my heart did pirouettes.
I folded it away for one subdued,
'Twas velvet soft, and blue or purple hued;
So comfortably it wore I near surrendered
To the platitudes and drabness it engendered,
And almost put my lifetime love to sleep.
'Twas then methought perhaps it's wise to keep
Two cloaks—the sombre one for all the times serene,
But occasionally—the gossamer and green.

Mary D. Sare

A Prayer for Peace

If we must kneel and kiss a wooden cross,
Or prostrate fall the sodden earth to meet,
Or bathe a black man's blistered feet,
Or of our most loved treasures suffer loss,
These are but the figments of the floss
Of humbleness 'twill take to first repeat
Our prayer for peace. Then, help us quickly to unseat
The bigotry of power and all the cloven dross
That we have woven into fabrics of the nations.
Make us, O God, aware of many gentle peoples standing by
Without a wish beyond the rights of their creations:
To breathe, to pray, to love, and oh, to cry
For a "sleep and a forgetting" of the fearful depredations
That men contrive today to make men die.

Mary D. Sare

Mockingbird

I heard him in the early morning hours
Before the sun arose. His timid song
Came trickling from the ancient oak that towers
Above its neighbor trees; then full and strong
It came cascading down as daylight roused
The field and meadow, and through hot noontide
While many woodland creatures slept or drowsed,
Till evening came and day had all but died.
Then in a song I'd heard the woodthrush sing,
In tiny kinglet's whistle, robin's trill
And twittering of swallows on the wing,
His accents rippled down the twilit hill.
It seemed that all the woodland's varied note
Had made a channel of his tiny throat.

Cordelia Spitzer

First Critic

Did Adam laugh
When God created
A giraffe in pleasure
Or derision
You know he did
Holding his belly he yelled
What is it
Both echoes circle this globe still
God annoyed said
I only create
You name and explain
Then made a crane.

Ruth Torbert

Questions

Fearing fame with a servile tense
Fear, yet attracted
I creep out at dusk
With a long bright pole to prod
At the glittering coiled and lethal creature.
Mine to capture perhaps,
Yet who wants the sleazy thing?
Well I do, I think I do.
How was it with you, Sappho?
Worth it?

Ruth Torbert

Nature Poem

Let me show you through the garden
The waterfall is sure to fall today
Hold your breath for seven simple steps
Then leap in cautious ecstasy
While last night's dream lingers
Over into morning
Turning roses green with thoughts
Unbecoming to a rose
Giving sustenance to insistent insects
Housed also near the waterfall
When it chooses to fall
Feebly or if not joyously then
In a manner that might be called boisterous
Perfect control at all times
Being, if not impossible, undesirable.

Ruth Torbert

Pan

Women dance
Up the hill
The bold moon rises
On the crest
They pose
A brown man sings
His staccato hooves
Beat the tempo
Rain drops a curtain
Over the moon
Running
Laughter
I too am running.

Ruth Torbert

Her Tornado

Panting
Damp and plump
She did not swoon
Nor flee from the funnel
Of cloud containing cows
And timber trash
But in a pleading crouch
Reached for the vortex.
It was a piquant chance
To travel.

Ruth Torbert

Spots

The centipedes in yellow yarn
Crawl over the wall
Through vast creative clutter.

Spots and blots form and mingle
Making a pattern
Without thought for that blot.

While that spot inebriated cries
I was happier alone
All this glitter

Is a snare
Beyond the Grand Teton's trail
Trailing after battered love.

Ruth Torbert

Surely Short

Seeing his great neck arched for loving
I inexperienced held his mane not shoving
And clambered high ungracefully
We raced our ribbons flowing to the sea
We swam for days then rested on a swell
Floating back guided by a bell
That chimed adventure's for the young
Well I am young or is this tongue
Babbling one of age that came upon me
While I slept decades away full fitfully
Under a moon gone mad again
Indifferently illuminating a season of pain.

Ruth Torbert

Witches

Watching for witches
In the lunar light
We float face up
In a salty slush pit
Coated with crystals
Soaring naked near a shadow
Cast by significant sharp forms
Climbing on currents bent on
Wrecking impudent intruders
A door swings over the pool
Topcoated footsteps stumble
Beyond a damp breeze
From another land
You are swaying in a tree
Top singing
Bent earthly ones plod past
Deaf
Soon snow filters under weary eyelids.

Ruth Torbert

My Brothers

My brother whose white hair
Once was red said his fingernails
Mourned with printer's ink
But kneading french bread
Took care of that
It was good bread too
But black and white of the printed page
Are for just some days
Most days we like the fruity
Colors like avacado green
And tangerine or again
The money colors like
Silver gold and mint green.
My other brother whose white hair
Also once was red said
His heart bled for the armadillos
That were persecuted in Amarillo
But I consider him peculiar in that respect
Since he might as well be bleeding
For the visionary viscera.

Ruth Torbert

Indiana Home

There stands the house within its ancient trees,
The lane curves downward gated from the road,
The birds still shake the orchard like a breeze
Above the brook where it has always flowed;
These friendly fields that were so large and far
To childish feet that knew their earth so long,
Lie smaller in their hedges than they are
Beside a highway's noisy rush and throng.

Their vassalship is now another's care;
Here changing scenes bring changing lives to dwell;
But I shall hear, when evening is aware
Of rain foreshadowed in an early gloom,
The muffled drafts of cattle at the well;
Smell clover in the lavender of bloom.

Margaret Trusler

Great Teacher

Words are the bright small coin of gratitude—
Copious, inexpensive. The thing that costs
Is indebtedness, not simply to be viewed
As exchange payable. One who exhausts
His treasuries to stock a hungry mind,
Hungry with hunger ever unfulfilled
Except this other share, offers the kind
Of service no one ever gave or willed
More than the teacher who never comes to terms
With compromise, but dropping the essential word,
Chastens, corrects, inspires, at last confirms
High effort—a burning-glass in the sun,
Thanked across the years for being such a one!

Margaret Trusler

Garden

When spring is a wild white freedom with hair unbound,
And soil once winter-tight is loose with birth,
There is no little plot of tended ground
Where I am led,
From bush to flower bed,
A foster mother to a square of earth.

I bring no shininess of spade or trowel
To grub the weed roots out and split the loam;
My fingers are as useless as the owl
In daylight glare;
I own no gardener's ware
To trellis vines and make them stay at home.

I watch the gradual tracery of fern
That will be foliage when it is grown,
And berry bushes as they lightly turn
From fagot sheaves
To a shadowing of leaves
Through white bouquets of blossom fruit-sown.

The paintbrush bursts to tiny solid fires;
The pentstemons, blown long and thin as glass,
Receive the woolly-legged insect fliers;
They pause and sup
In Mariposa's cup,
And blue harebells that empty toward the grass.

Spring is my garden . . .

Margaret Trusler

Selected Poems by Other Entrants

GEORGE W. ALLISON
WARREN ANDREW
ROWENA APPLEGATE
EDWARD LEE BARKER
BOB BASLER, JR.
RILEY BERTRAM
CLIFF BYERS, JR.
TIMOTHEUS H. CARSON
PATRICIA ANNA CONSTABLE
LOIS ANNE COWLES
WINIFRED E. EADS
MARY E. GIBSON
JAY GOULD
CONSTANCE GROGAN
MEREDITH R. HASKETT
GRANT HENDERSON
JAMES C. JEWELL
STEVEN KERN
CANDUS M. LANG
ROBERT LONG
ALMA C. MAHAN
ELIZABETH MARSHALL
MARY McNORTON
REX PETERS
JAMES L. ROSS
BARBARA SIEMINSKI
MARY E. SIMMONS
MAUD COURTNEY WADDELL
STEVEN C. WARD
MARK E. WYSS
GLADYS S. YOUNG

Maine Shore

How cold this ocean is!
It surges in great swells
That rise, break into combers
That rush landwardly
Under this low gray sky!
As they near this beachless shore,
The waves heave, rear, hiss—
Then cast themselves endlessly
In green water, foam, and misty spume
Across these barren granite spits
Where Maine, from her dark forests,
Thrusts long bony fingers
Into this cold thrashing sea.
One's oilskin wets with spatter
From the wind-blown spray
That leaves the taste of salt
Upon the lips.

George W. Allison

War Memorial

"Dulce et decorum est pro patria"
to die; so in the center of our town
there stands a tower high.
And always when the sun goes down,
the white stones turn to bloody red
and it is all too plain,
these are the bones of men who bled—
and I am surely sane.

The living leave the somber scene; they make
all haste to fly; and never do they once
look back upon that tower high.
I know they fear to face their Dead
when night is drawing nigh;
for always as the darkness comes
I see that bloody stain;
and it is all too clear to me
that *they* are sons of Cain—
and I am surely sane.

Warren Andrew

Ghosts

Tonight I burned my memories. I sat for hours,
Searching for some magic in the embers' glow
To change reality and cause heartache to disappear
In the twilight beyond the curtain of gently falling snow.
Hours of unchecked tears born at the fountain of frustration!
Reluctantly I wield the poker and add fuel
To the flames, as though hastening destruction
Will bring oblivion to memories both blessed and cruel.
Can the greedy flames destroy the image of tortured souls,
The fragmented rose petals, symbol of lost dreams and sentiment?
Like Meshach, Shadrach, Abednego they march on the bier of hope,
Residents of my heart that are permanent.
Dawn heralds a new day. Old pains, fresh tears
Greet the metamorphosis in the smouldering ashes.
Remain the pictures indelible to eradication.
Anguished faces reappear in uninvited flashes;
Ghosts prowl the shadowed corners, futile forgetfulness;
The flames have completed their ineffectual task.
My heart did not vacate its tenants as the empty box,
But the world will see serenity assume its concealing mask;
Days will find fulfillment in service to God and man;
Moloch will be defeated in quest of the Macedonian cry;
But what shall I do in the lonely quiet hours
With ghosts of memories that refuse to die?

Rowena Applegate

In Normandy's Rows

A farmer plows the bones
  The bones of the Wehrmacht
Corporal's coal-scoop helmet
  Rusted and black . . .
He uncovers the history
  With his poorman's plow,
Ground once stepped with
  Heavy boots and grinding
Tracks of steel, long erased
  By rains and grass . . .
The upturned soil, the earth
  Yields its traces of eras
Passed in splintered hulks of
  Rifle butts, of cartridges
  Unspent.
Some would say he opened a wound
  In the earth and the ground
Cried out . . . the terror it had
  Felt in that the year of
Forty-four . . . year of blood
  And fire of funeral pyres of
Armies.
  He plows open a diary of a
Day concealed; he stirs the
  Sunken trunk of a warrior fallen
A score of years gone by . . .
  A young man's bones . . . a son,
A father, fixed in unmarked grave,
  His day spent for a cause,
And life consumed . . .
  There is only the twitter of
Birds and the wind in the hedgerows
  From afar, as an old man plows
Where young men have fallen . . .

Edward Lee Barker

The Hard Part of Easy

In my misty night of morning
In my fleeting black of white
In my falling star of memory
You haven't left me quite

So my foggy sad of laughter
Tells my kidnapped molded grin
That my keyhole sense of happiness
Should ask you back again

But my rope's-end ball of yarn
Fills my burlap bag of sorrow
And it warns me of the price I'll owe—
The pay-me-back of borrow

For some cracker-crumb security
In a charcoal sketch of life
And the waiting part of wanting
It just isn't worth the price

Bob Basler, Jr.

Cantata Per Un Castrato

Of course, they must have their bells ringing God.
And who would mind the loss of one war cry?
They demand a FEW.
What wind could blow that candle out to die?
I have no nose for stench of burning rod.
But they NEED angels.
O wandering manhood not yet blossomed,
O boy who waits upon the threshold's door,
I cry blood for you,
For when the deed is done you shall be poor.

Your soul knows, though you may not, what's ransomed.
Poor little clipped bird.
Only the creek-clear song notes, learned and proud,
Understand the plan to keep them in you
For their own ear's joy.
Tolling a fate that comes to yet but few,
Bells, bells, bells. Sweet, sweet, bells. Ring long, ring loud.
Reverberate sin.
Through the veil of years, I can not reach out
And wipe the blood from your innocent years
Nor stop the scyther.
I hold you now, and gather your new tears,
And through time, still wince from hearing your shout
Of pain for art's sake.

Many notes in time and song fall before
The robbers are gone from the kingdom for
Arts and melody.
Many deeds in time cried art, yet still warred
In robes of butchers and the swords they wore.
I sing back to you,
It will be centuries, dear boy, until
They judge you not needed to pray or chant
Or to cry Godward.
You are doomed to dangle on your penchant,
For history can only slow instill
Rights for each man's own.
I cry for your created voice is lost
Unrecorded to ancient wind and ears
Not yet knowing light
And through all time and through all years, your years,
No men shall know the price the knife has cost,
Yet we loved you, boy.

Riley Bertram

Marks on White

Full stops and commas in the snow,
Dark pods on brittle stalks they go.

I watch them in the bone-bleak light—
Across a wilderness of white . . .

Writing their hieroglyphic words:
Poor cold inconsequential birds!

Cliff Byers, Jr.

Bleakness

The frozen beams, knobby with last year's nests,
Are flaked with hoar frost. Fusty cobwebs break
Under the cornice, while the idle quest
Of wind is the only sound that breaks
The winter's silence. Slender straps of weed
Sully the barn's side. Here the field mice make
Swift, fearful journeys for a mite of seed—
Searching each cleft and cranny urgently;
Bats hang like empty bagpipes. Darkness suddenly.

Cliff Byers, Jr.

All Is . . .

Distance is all.
All is distance.
All distance is.

The distance of the tormented valleys.
The womb of the earth is stuffed.
The distance of mutilated suburbs.

The eyesore of an abandoned car on a sleek, fat street.
The distance, sometimes, of a few yards.
The distance of the hillside cemetery wounded with the
rawness of new trenches.

The flowers will fade on the mountains.
The toys will spill their stuffing and break their springs.
Hideous detritus, this distance.

Everybody must look and shout?
Must there be no sentiment?
Must all feel upon their skin the great dark eyes of final
distance?

Distance is all.
The uncaring distance of people.
But, above all, the uncaring of distant people.

Cliff Byers, Jr.

Voices in the Forest

(The Apple Tree)

Redder than Sapphire in noonday light
Or the fire of an inflamed heart
Bolder than starlings in morning flight
Is the hue that my gems impart.
Eye them!
Weigh them!
Vie them!
Charged with the beauty of Season's charm
And the power of Kings' delight.

(The Pear Tree to the Pine)

Behold me, behold me!
I vie with the finest.
The gems that infold me
Are indeed the divinest.
See how glittering they bedazzle me.
Tell me, simple tree,
Is it well with thee?
Dressed in shoddy green
How indeed thou repinest.

(The Chestnut)

I am the lilting chestnut queen.
I seek your lauding clamour.
You in your horrid frock of green,
Have you not seen such glamour
Of velvet white and eastern silk
Of royal lace as pale as milk
Which now my form enamour?

(The Song of the Dogwood)

Have you not seen a gownlet
Of more enthralling beauty
It dazzles the bright starlet

And scorns her astral duty?
I sway I dance in the morning breeze;
I sprinkle gossamer on the trees
They marvel at my beauty!

(The Cherry Blossom Lady to the Pine)

I the cherry blossom lady
Come to show my regal hue.
See my pink and flaky tresses
Thrown against the skylight blue.
Tell me, tell me, little neighbor,
Why not join the buoyant scene,
Damsel moping in the woodlands
Dressed in such a simple green?

(The Pine)

I know a mystery!
That sets my heart to dance and song
In my short history.
Eternities my green prolong
The gentle wind has talked to me
In whispers filled with quiet glee
And I must sway in music all day long.
I do not know who brings the spring and fall,
But joy has taken hold on me.
And when the last wind blows to silence all
I'll have my song inside of me.

(Jack Frost)

I am Jack Frost.
See me!——Feel me!
I chill the ground.
Ah, none hears me.
I paint the post that holds the fence.
Summer is lost,——Autumn comes hence!
They who today in crimson bound,
Tomorrow shall be dull dull brown.
They'll counter me, in their last round.

I come!
They pay the season's cost.
Two words they'll sigh,
Jack Frost! Jack Frost!

(North Wind)

You see, I send my armies from the North
To freeze the verdant woodlands and the plain
And they who seek to hurl my Legions forth
Alas prevail their weary souls in vain.

Look on the pine tree, you creatures,
For she is crowned with the rainbow.
Look on her shimmering train.
I've made her your queen
For in such transfixed awe you shall remain!

Timotheus H. Carson

Haiku on Friendship

You cannot will it;
Like a flowering tendril,
root and seed meet soil.

Patricia Anna Constable

Images from *Justine* by Lawrence Durrell

Time shot. Flung. Out from a prism rose.
    Music rose. Time. Time. Time.
    and Being was still.

And we climbed to God
    where morning was
    and stony flowered grasses,
    free, and goat-loved, lived.

Alexandria is a magic word,
    a harpsichord,
a prayer filtered through a silent,
    stained glass spectrum.
A home at last.

Crosses atop climaxes of devotion.
    A counterpoint to death.
Light from the universe converges there,
    on white houses where hills declare
        in triumph—"The Sea"!

And music, the soul's voice,
    surely was delivered there,
    antithesis to pain
    in infinite form.

Man is a mirror, the moment a snowflake,
    and hell is universally known.

Lois Anne Cowles

Resistance Overcome

Thin trees stretched tall and parallel,
    angled from the ground,
in the woods snowed with moonlight
    where life fell fearless to its sounds,
rustling a refusal of Fall to leave,
    begging winter's chill to stay another hour,
ignoring its touch
    like the rattle of childhood's toys,
when growth beckons rest.

And the moon reflected the sun's bright light,
    making believe it was not night,
and the mystery drew us yielding
    for even the dried persimmons would not fall,
and the white rock of the road
    descended and curved into meadows,
banked by startling hills,
    gently bearing music.

And the dried grasses leaned
    like the beach grasses green,
and the leaves of the trees
    softly trembled still.
As we stood in the feeling
    that life is worth pain,
    my love was glad
    you shared this moment too.

Lois Anne Cowles

Exuberant Exclamation

Steeped in expectation,
I waited for you to visit me,
to take me shyly on your knee.
I waited with roses at my waist,
pasted on
with marginal distaste,
disgraced entirely
because my expectation
was entirely too exuberant.
I should have been like you—
—sophisticated and worldly-wise,
wearing nonchalance as disguise
to hide the persistence of my eyes.

Winifred E. Eads

If You Should Come Today

If you should come today
I would take two cups from the shelf
and dust them inside out
until two spheres of emptiness
shared no sphere of doubt.
I would put a ribbon in my hair
because you used to like one there.
I should cut the day in shreds
with the scissors of a hoping
and if I heard your knock,
I think I wouldn't even tremble
but only open the door
until the hinges gasped
and take you in my arms.

Winifred E. Eads

Square Trees

In the valley of my libido
  limpid waters flow,
and square trees grace the gardens
  where white petunias grow.

Bathed in psychic scented consciousness,
  naked truth concealed,
the square trees clasp in silence
  memoirs the id revealed.

Erase my valley of ecstasies
  change the water's flow,
the wholeness of my being,
  square trees and all must go.

Mary E. Gibson

Rediscovery

An eon ago,
I rode a silk white stallion,
across the desert sands,
along the Gulf of Guinea,
and long forgotten lands.
Like the robin searches
when summer loses caste,
the haunting visions clung to
are remnants of the past.
I found the Indus Valley
and grasped a style unknown;
I met the mighty Khmers,
and called their souls, my own.
As the prodigal returns,
spent with being free,
my glimpse in time's great mirror
reflected only me.
An eon ago.

Mary E. Gibson

Metamorphosis

My soul was so hungry,
So hungry in me,
For the sight of the mountains,
The smell of the sea;

So hungry my soul was
For friends that were fine,
For a house and a garden
That I could call mine;

For one day without worry,
One day without haste,
One day without torture
Of debt to be faced.

So hungry my soul was
To let one day pass
Just lying and dreaming
Alone on the grass

By the brook that skips laughing
Down from the hill,
And creeps on its hands and knees
Under the mill.

So I sought for a purse full
Of gold, for they said
That would buy me the day
And my soul could be fed.

Year on year, dawn till dark,
I labored for gold,
Till my voice was metallic
And my blood was cold.

At last the day came
When my soul I could nurse;
But I sought it and found
It had turned to a purse.

Jay Gould

Abandoned

The wooden walls of the
Fort creak with eerie tone,
And inside—
A name written on a stone.

Something beyond a soul's
Comprehension lies there—
The forsaken feeling that
None is to care.

Silence conquers the
Place of the Dead
While on the outside
Chaos rules, and the world
            Is Red
With the blood of war.

A perverse wind
            Ripples the torn
Banner
            and flees
To return no more.

Constance Grogan

The Poet

He has a perspective wealth cannot buy.
Some look with disdain at a squirming worm—
He sees tomorrow's butterfly.

Meredith R. Haskett

Futility

He would not know defeat; he stirred
The embers of an ashy past,
And when a wisp of smoke appeared
He added fuel he thought would last
This time. He blew an ember to a glow
And suddenly, a twig afire,
Enthusiasm raged, and he
Piled on the fuel, a whole lot higher,
And killed the spark; he smothered it,
But like a soldier true—and tried—
He kept on starting little fires
That never burned. One day he died.

Grant Henderson

The Modern Ozymandias

The haze wears off and fog rolls on,
Slow moving across damp green blankets
Broken alone by rectangles of earth.
Accenting each is stone, cold stone;
Occasionally a cross,
Punctuated by an angel cherub,
A frozen sepulchral smile
Upon cracked, chapped lips.

How long must this last?
Must we look on the works in decay?
Nearby, the lone and level grounds stretch far away.

James C. Jewell

Quiet Town

I want to be where it is very still
I do not want to hear even a cricket's shrill
Nor a songbird from the wood
Nor a stir of wind along the hill
But I would not mind
If far away
A church bell were softly ringing
Some sense of unsought absolution bringing
Not urging
Me to pray
I would like to be immersed in warmth
When night's shadows darken
And the stillness
Across the meadow stealing
Healing day's hardness and brass
Like the shadows that are creeping
To settle in my mind.

Steven Kern

Magic Spring

If dandelions are just weeds to you,
Not lollipops stuck in the dew;
If the moon is just a moon,
No gypsy girl will dance and swoon.

If a jaybird's just a jay,
No little clown will perform all day.
If an apple tree is just a tree,
And not a heaven for a bee;

If a kitten's just a cat,
Something that you never pat;
If dew drops are just drops of rain,
Not jewels strung on a string;

If you would rather sleep past dawn,
Never watch a tiny fawn;
Nor hear the morning carolers sing;
Brother! You have missed the spring.

Candus M. Lang

Sleep Soft, My Son

Sleep soft, my son, all nestled snug and safe in
soft brown earth, where I myself did lay you down.

Sleep soft and dream of childhood's dreams, the kind
that only children know, and all the rest of us can
only wish to live again.

Sleep soft through all the winter time of death
and wake, I pray thee, only in the warm green Spring
of GOD.

Robert Long

Light and Shadow

To the young
Death is a little green Martian
From an uncharted world.
Quick as a dangerous dream,
Quicker than cobra or coral
He snatches reluctant prey
From a life of pleasure.

To the old
Death is a familiar friend.
Quiet as a windless day,
Quiet as approaching night
He strolls close by in the Autumn
To promise peace as dry leaves fall
On paths secluded and strange.

Alma C. Mahan

Precious Garden

Loving Lord, Bless our
Garden of Children.

Plant their roots deep in the
Soil of holiness.

Turn their faces to the
Warmth of Your love.

Quench their thirst with the
Nectar of Your graces.

Guard them from the
Weeds of wickedness.

Protect them from the
Thistles of temptation.

Render their souls fruitful
With growth toward You.

Elizabeth Marshall

Pursuit

Day is a child
Whirling with the wind
Washing in the rain
Warmed by the heart of the sun.

Twilight is day's mother.
Suddenly she's there,
Touching fingers to his eyelids,
Kissing starlight in his hair.

Elizabeth Marshall

Solace

The commonplace checks my body;
By duties I'm bound to the real.
    My trammeled self
    Cleans a pantry shelf
But my soul will never be still.

'Tis futile to dream of freedom
With this thing and that thing to do.
    But I smile at my task;
    In whimsies I bask,
For my soul is away in the blue.

To covet the life of adventure
Dispels peace and chafes the will.
    Though duties surround,
    I'm happy I've found
That my soul need never stay still.

Mary McNorton

Another poem by Mary McNorton is included in the humorous poetry section.

Bittersweet Addiction

When first I chose the poet's pen
A searing flame burned in my mind,
For I was blessed above all men
The mystery of the muse to find.

Oh, for a while the search was joy,
For fancy is a winsome lass;
But fame stood like a bully boy
To block the road that I would pass.

When other matters, live and real,
Would throw a dampness on the glow,
Why, I'd profess I did not feel
The aching void that hurt me so.

I thought the fire would surely die,
But reckoned not a latent will,
And while I'm much too big to cry,
Alas! the embers burn me still.

Rex Peters

Pagan Sky

Under the darkness of clear cold skies
Chilling frost cracks crisp beneath my feet.
From glittering skies with darkening horizons
I sense the eeriness of winter's night
Beckoning me to worlds not known,
Worlds with amorphous thrones—awaiting!
The chill of night steepens the mystery of far-off lights.
The sense of presence of an age that's past
Transmits me to centuries when others strolled the night.
How did they these far-off lights explain
With a less-thinking more primitive brain?
Can we, with the burdensome wisdom of accumulated time
(when all our knowing yields perplexity),
Solve more than they—knowing more, wondering more,
having more doubt?
A doubt amassed by centuries of discontent.
Oh, for a Pagan mind to face a Pagan sky!

James L. Ross

Why?

Through doves of white, a vespered peace
Comes winging down to me—
But I evade its restful fleece
And flee Eternity.

Confined by sorrow, sin, and shame
I dare not move away:
The sacrifice of sweet acclaim
Is far too much to pay . . .

Barbara Sieminski

Spring Winds

I like the feel of soft spring winds
upon my skin
for that is when I'd like to lose
all inhibitions,
and make the wind my dress.
It makes me dream of clean-tipped hills
free to the sky,
Where I might rise above the world
with upstretched arms
to catch a star.

Mary E. Simmons

The Friendly Things

The humming kettle on the fire—
The wind and pine-trees' age-old choir—
A book to read and also lend—
A welcome letter from a friend—
The faithful dog beside your chair—
The kitten romping on the stair—
A cricket's never ending tune—
Some fragrant flowers in the room.
The big old maple's spreading arms—
The moon and stars' bewitching charms—
The lowing cattle near the barns—
The stirring joy each birdsong brings.
I find the simple, homely things
Can ease the heart until it sings.

Maud Courtney Waddell

April

and April is nice if you
 don't think twice how
 things that come also
 must go

for April is laughing and
 fresh, clean air that blows
 in your face and scatters
 your hair

and April is mud but mud
 is fun and sometimes
 blood (but, Mom, we won)

and sometimes April just doesn't
 end much like a
 poem and much like
 a friend

Steven C. Ward

A Leaf Chases Me

A leaf chases me across
the sidewalk
along with a Boy
late for supper
We are on the corner and the light
says in white letters
WAIT
The Boy looks both ways; there
are no cars coming.
He runs across the street;
his mother is calling.
My mother does not call
and
My foot toys with a rock while
I wait for the sign
to change to
WALK.

Steven C. Ward

Death

Death is a squirrel
bloody on the road
with a walnut nearby.

Steven C. Ward

i am sunday afternoon

i am sunday afternoon
        raining
    just out of bed
    plagued with pimples and a gap
        between my teeth
    hair everywhere and infant beard;
        i have not shaved
my old shirt
    turtle-neck and black
        black hair and beard
old levi's and no shoes
    hoping that someone will tell me
        to get dressed
    to shave
        to look presentable
because she likes me
    dressed and shaved
        presentable
but today i have only my poems
    and today my poems are silent

Steven C. Ward

Mongoloid

Peeping Thomas
Fills his eyes.
It seems funny;
Hideously hilarious
"Nimble Norman"
Simple poorman
Beastly lamb
Unfinished man.

His mother's son,
His mother's sin,
His mother's maimed pain
Plays with clumsy blocks
And eats coloring books.

Drooling mouth
Dead tooth
In a booth,
Come one
Come all
After all
These years,
Tears,
Cries,
And lies,
He dies
Because
He can't
Eat soup with his fingers.
He will always
Need;
He will never
Succeed.
And so on
So you say.

Hear now
Then
My old man
Face tan
Running away from
"Nothing,"
Norman will
Someday feed
Your melancholy psyche.
And Tom,
He will be
No more
Than a simple sadling
Sipping scummy
Skimmed milk.
When Tom tries
To climb
Over
The great, gray, grate, gate
To Norman's land,
He will find
Soap
On his rotten rope.

Please pray
For those
Who chose
To oppose
Norman,
The beastly lamb
Unfinished man.

Mark E. Wyss

Pay at the Next Troll Bridge

I sit ingrown
At home,
All alone,
And groan.

I wonder why
The reason why
Men live to die
Might imply
That life can fly.

I need no one
To know who won,
If the sun had spun,
Or if someone
Had fun.

I need stalls
And blistered walls
And tragic falls
With bloody calls
And deep fried crystal balls.

I'm a negative fugitive
Out to outlive
My primitive
Positive relative.

My own private world
Never wore old
And isn't a whorled,
War old, whore held
World.

The circus is in town.
Look at the clown
Drown in his brown gown.
He is a noun with a frown.

They think me queer;
Jab and jeer,
And even fear
When I am near.
I am sincere
And will always sneer
At those who come here
To leer.
I don't think they want me here!

Don't fret;
No sweat;
Just threat;
No net or bayonet.
Should I set
My bet
And fall in debt;
Or get?

Begone!
Move on!
Half pawn
Part swan,
Swim upon
The Amazon.

Hermit on stage,
Bandage your heritage.
Begin your pilgrimage
And pay at the next troll bridge.

Mark E. Wyss

Paths Are for the Aged

She scorned a waiting, easy path,
    To measure and explore
The depths of cold white fluffiness
    Heaped there beside my door;
The need to do so evidenced
    By new red boots she wore.

That wayside mystery of white
    Has vanished long ago.
The small red boots—I see them still
    In memory sweet to know;
They symbolize the untried way
    A pioneer should go.

Gladys S. Young

Selected Humorous Entries

ALICE S. CAMPBELL
JAMES W. GRIMES
BERNIECE T. HISER
MILDRED LEISURE IRVIN
MARY LOCKE JOHNSTON
SISTER M. ISABELL LAMPE
MARY McNORTON
HARRY C. SNIDER
CAROL B. WEINBERG

Maturity

Since time is creeping up on me
And I cannot retract it,
It seems the thing for me to do
Is know my age and act it.

Alice S. Campbell

In the Spring

"In the spring a young man's fancy,"
The old, old, story goes.
But what of him, the elder male,
Or is there one who knows?

I've investigated thoroughly,
And through my own research,
Have found he turns to gardening
Or catching eager perch.

Oh, yes! A glint of former springs
May flash within his eyes.
But there to squelch the tiny spark
A sea of calmness lies.

James W. Grimes

Reluctant Hostess

I wrote, "Come up and see me soon;"
I was just plain mountain polite.
Back she wrote, "May I bring a friend?
We'll be there Saturday night."

I said, "I've got the cutest homemade house;"
It was just old mountain brag.
She cried, "I'd be tickled to death to see it;
Here, James, load up my bag!"

I remarked, "I've frying chickens,
Just roaming in my lot."
She sighed, "I'll help you eat them tomorrow night;
And I like my biscuits hot!"

Now, when I'm acting hostess-like,
As if I were a guest collector,
Lest I perhaps be misunderstood,
I wear a lie-detector.

Berniece T. Hiser

Solomon Swiggett

(This poem is from the book *Cumberland* now being written. This store was actually at Middletown, Indiana.)

Old Solomon Swiggett, that luckless man,
Got here with a crack in his frying pan,
Some sullen hens, and bless his lot,
He lost the lid to his coffee pot.
His ax was dull and his horse was slow,
And his brindle cow just wouldn't go,
So he walked around this lonesome plot
And he shrugged and sighed, and said, "Why not?"

Now he couldn't chop a hickory tree
Or walnut, or oak, that's plain to see,
But a stand of chestnut loomed close by
So he said to his ax, "Let's give 'er a try!"
He hacked them down, both great and small
And he said, "By gum, they'll make a wall!"
They were wopper-jawed and not too high,
But they cut the wind and kept him dry.

The shakes he split were a little thick—
He was mighty short on arithmetic—
But he held them fast with some sturdy pegs,
And the hens moved in and laid some eggs.
Maybe you think he wasn't proud!
He hung the door and laughed aloud;
Then he milked the cow and slapped his leg
And nailed a board on top of a keg.

Now that's the way the store began
That Boston knew and Hindustan;
Old Solomon Swiggett opened his door
With little more than the clothes he wore.
The frying pan and the coffee pot
Went out with his shoes and a bag of shot
And when he'd sold everything down to the floor,
He climbed on his horse and went for more.

The business grew and he bought some land
But folks just never could understand
Why he kept that store of chestnut logs
There by the swamp with the snakes and frogs,
For that cabin sprouted every spring—
(A chestnut does that, silly thing!)
But Solomon trimmed her, fling and flog,
And dreamed by the fire with a mug of grog.

Well, riches came and a house of brick
Stood tall and proud by the muddy crick;
There were porches too, and a great front door,
A wife and young 'uns, three or four.
A fine post road climbed over the hill
With the stage horns blowing loud and shrill.
He shrugged and built a fancy store
With glass and counters and shelves galore.

But when spring came and the chestnut logs
In the cabin sprouted down by the bogs,
Old Solomon trimmed 'er, fling and flog
And dreamed by her fire with a cup of grog.

Mildred Leisure Irvin

Mud Pies

Sing a song of make-believe.
A tot in pinafore
Bakes her mud pies in the sun,
Beside my kitchen door.

Sing a song of stolen soil.
A flower bed tells a tale
Of having been invaded
By a spoon and water pail.

Sing a song of make-believe,
Of water that is tea,
Of sand that's really sugar
And sweet as sweet can be.

Sing a song of rolling pins
And pans for mixing dough,
Of finished pies upon a board,
All baking in a row.

Sing a song of make-believe.
Of dollies that agree
That leaves are really pennies
Found growing on a tree.

Sing a song of happy days
When life was full of fun.
Sing a song of make-believe
And mud pies in the sun.

Mary Locke Johnston

To an Earthworm

Slimy, slithering worm so thin,
Scarce a toothpick, soft of skin,
Wriggling, squirming, here and there,
Groveling on the ground for air;
You remind me, for 'twas told,
That to mountains you seem bold,
For you crumble earthy soil,
And from rain-floods won't recoil;
To the husbandman, a friend,
To the fisher's hook, an end,
Yet like Python must resign
When Apollo's sword and shine
Shrink you to a scrawny thread
And you're doomed among the dead.

Sister M. Isabell Lampe

The Well-Disposed Cat

I pummel and pull her
Tail and I wool her—
    She purrs.

I berate and scold her
Or tenderly hold her—
    She purrs.

I stroke her or strike her
She's sure that I like her—
    She purrs.

A welcome transition
Were my disposition—
    Like hers.

Mary McNorton

I Bit into a Worm

I bit into a worm today;
A Baldwin on the ground
Housed in the chamber where he lay
And munched the walls around.

What chances for philosophy
On Death and Fate unbending,
When he looked up in time to see
The pearly gate descending!

Harry C. Snider

The Funeral

The minister was there in black;
The bearers of the pall,
The tightly pressed, fan-waving pack,
The choir against the wall.

A field of flowers was ranged along
The altar, hushed and dim;
The organ's pulse was firm and strong,
When someone rolled a hymn.

And then among the churchyard trees,
Of cedar and of pine,
The final, graveside obsequies
Were simple, solemn, fine.

But now the people turn away
As shades of night draw near.
Am I ungrateful if I say
It's really cold down here!

Harry C. Snider

The Ph.D.

We watched a laboratory rat
Complete his education:
His school was a dispenser that
Would yield a pellet ration.

He passed by proving he could think
And manage food-obtaining.
The school diploma, signed in ink,
Would certify his training!

And, then, I pondered on the fate
This graduate would find,
When lab assistants raised the gate
And poked him from behind.

To make his education pay,
To use the credits earned,
His food must *always* come the way
That he, in school, has learned.

But, what if Life's an automat,
With food containers, clever,
Each gadget, there, demanding that
He learn a *different* lever!

What profit, then, his special skill
To work one certain bar?
Define the issue as you will,
He's *specialized* too far!

If food is free, no bar to move
To get what suits his taste,
Such lax economy must prove
His time in school a waste!

Indeed, his chance is more than good
To find such habitat;
It seems that easy livelihood
Comes natural to a rat!

And, by the way, this rat's degree,
His academic crown,
Of course, he got a Ph.D.;
He Pushed the Handle Down!

Harry C. Snider

Old Age Security

She used to peer beneath her bed,
Each night at pillow time,
The gesture of a maid unwed
To fend an amorous crime.

In later years, less supple cords
Supplanted sinews wiry;
She pushed a broom across the boards
To make the same inquiry.

But, now, she lets the caution drop;
Too plainly it appears
That Time, alone, has put a stop
To all her former fears.

For, when a maid's too old to kneel
And has to use a broom,
She really has no cause to feel
A man is in her room.

Harry C. Snider

The Wail of the Warm-blooded Weakling

"The Northern Lights have seen queer sights"—
That's Service, as you recall—
But, if I ever went to the land he meant,
They'd see the queerest of all!

I'm a tenderfoot who never would put
His head in an ice igloo;
The Eskimo does that, I know,
But I'd turn solid blue!

The Arctic storm would find me warm
But not in a snow-banked cove;
I'd be content in my nylon tent
Embracing a benzine stove!

I'd pack canned heat for the grub I'd eat—
No frozen beans or spuds!
My snow attire would be half wire,
All battery-heated duds!

I'd need no gun for food or fun;
That sport has little appeal!
I have no use for bear or moose,
And gag at the thought of seal!

Were I to mush over ice and slush
With dogs in a tugging line,
The huskies' wail on that lonely trail
Would never be heard over mine!

No Malamute gal as trail-bed pal—
That holds no charm for me!
If ever she rolled me out in the cold,
I'd freeze like Sam McGee!

So I'll forego the Arctic floe
And all such polar scenes;
That life's too rough; I'm thrilled enough
By outdoor magazines!

Harry C. Snider

Teaching by "Pattern Drill"

Two cavemen sat on a bulrush mat,
One day, when the World was young,
Content to munch on their wart hog lunch,
And talk in the caveman tongue.

With grunts and growls and velar vowels,
And clicks in the current convention,
They threaded through, this timeless two,
A weak and a strong declension.

For Opp was yearning for language learning,
While Ugg knew an alien speech,
And valued more than his verbal store
Was the *method* he used to teach!

He'd put Opp through a form or two,
Then go on a lingual bender,
By switching the tense, or changing the sense
Of person, number, and gender!

And so, all day, Ugg taught this way,
His school, a hole in a hill,
Neanderthal Man inventing the plan
We now call *pattern drill!*

Harry C. Snider

To Weave a Symphony

Now, Pegasus, again you loaf and wander.
Will you ever steady down and learn to stay
In stable here and not expect to play?
While I hear rhythms patterning, and ponder,
Why must you putter, browsing over yonder
Or even scamper haughtily away?
You must know that Clio comes this time of day.
You love to rhyme, but you seem even fonder
Of wasting hours. I give you feed and drink
Because I stand in urgent need of you
In every fevered syllable I write.
You whinny and draw nearer . . . form the link
With all the great Olympic retinue
To weave a symphony in black and white!

Carol B. Weinberg

ACKNOWLEDGMENTS

The editor wishes to thank the editors of various publications for the privilege of reprinting poems.

Constance Hunting's poems first appeared in the following publications: "The Perfectionist," "At Mrs. R's" in *Quartet*; "City Park: Spring," "Year-round," "Coming Home," "Minute Observations" (1,3,4,5) in *Sparrow*; "Afternoon of a Contemporary Poet," "A Dream of Heavenly Love and Redemption in the Wood" in *Poetry*; "Bird in Hand" in *Western Humanities Review*; "Miss Dickinson" in University of Massachusetts *Review.*

David F. Gladish's poems are reprinted by permission of the editors of the following publications: "Death Is Dreadful," *Epos*; "Lavov," *Accent.*

Ray Mizer's poems originally appeared in the following publications: "Confessions" in *Western Poet*; "Garden Hints": I in *Arizona Quarterly,* V in *Fiddlehead,* VI in *Poetry Digest,* VII, XII in *Flame,* XV in *Lynx*; "Poets, Readers, Critics": I in *Carolina Quarterly,* II, V, VIII in *College English,* III in *DePauw Magazine,* VII in *Midwest*; "Hover" in *Epos*; "Bell Weather" in *Carolina Quarterly;* "D.A.R.ling" in *Beloit Poetry Journal*; "First Manassas" in *Caravel.*

Arnold Lazarus's poems are reprinted by permission of the editors of the following publications: "A House Named Sylvia," *Saturday Review*; "Traveler's Agent," *Sparrow;* "Great Lakes Gothic," *Discourse;* "Decorations on a Japanese Fan," *College English;* "One Ticket, One Dance (a penny opera)," *English Journal.*

Joseph Colin Murphey's poems are reprinted by permission of the editors of the following publications: "That Morning and Evening Sun," "A Noise of Battle," "*Pieta* by Mantegna (1431-1506)," *Southwest Review*; "Ode to the Statue Who Found a Trade" and "Portrait of a Lady," *The Texas Quarterly.*

Daisy Stieber Squadra's "Fragments from Bethlehem" is reprinted by permission of *The Republic.* All other poems by Daisy Stieber Squadra are reprinted by permission of *The Christian Science Monitor.*

Willis Barnstone's poems are reprinted by permission of the editors of the following publications: "Kaminia-Hydra," *Greek Heritage*; "Standstill," New York *Times*; "Going Outside," *Antioch Review*; "Lapland," *The New Yorker.*

Jeanne Eagles McCormack's "The Orchard" is reprinted by permission of the editor of *Sparrow.*

Frances Brown Price's poems are reprinted by permission of the editors of the following publications: "The Slowly Shaping Heart," *The Poet,* Madras, India; "On Wings Barely Dry," *The Oregonian,* Portland, Oregon; "In What New Bethlehem," *Cyclo-Flame,* San Angelo, Texas; "Too Sad for Spring," *Green World,* Baton Rouge, Louisiana.

Earl Hughes's poems are reprinted by permission of the editors of the following publiiations: "Once I Was in New Orleans," *Caravan;* "Second-Growth Timber," *The Land*; "The Scoundrels," *Flame.*

Mary Roe's "Okefenokee" is reprinted from *American Bard.*

Margaret Trusler's "Indiana Home" was first published in *The World's Fair Anthology of Verse* in 1939.

Jay Gould's "Metamorphosis" is from the book *Hello, World,* copyright 1966, by Jay Gould, WOWO, Fort Wayne.

Meredith R. Haskett's "The Poet" is reprinted from the Indianapolis *News.*

Barbara Sieminski's "Why?" is reprinted from the 1967 Saint Francis College *Poetry.*

Mary E. Simmon's "Spring Winds" is reprinted from the Columbus *Evening Republican.*

Carol B. Weinberg's "To Weave a Symphony" was previously published in *The Haven Press* and also included in *Archives of the Heart* (1947) by Carol B. Weinberg.

It is understood that all of the poetry in this volume remains the property of the individual poet and may be published elsewhere without permission from the editor of *Indiana Sesquicentennial Poets.*